Alien Entities

Beings From Beyond

Alien Entities

Beings From Beyond

by
Dr. Lester Sumrall

LeSEA PUBLISHING COMPANY
South Bend, Indiana

ALIEN ENTITIES
ISBN 0-89274-320-4
Copyright © 1984
by Lester Sumrall Evangelistic Association.

3rd printing

Published by LeSEA Publishing Company
P.O. Box 12, South Bend, Indiana 46624

Contents

1
Introduction to Alien Entities

Nothing is more forceful or powerful than an idea whose time has come. I believe that the time has come for the truth to be told about alien entities. This is a subject that reaches deeper into the inner recesses of my spirit than I am capable of expressing. Every time I confront a person with emotional illness, my total spiritual capacity goes into orbit seeking to discover an answer to his need.

It would seem from the Gospel story that the Lord Jesus was intensely motivated by the same human need. This truth causes me to believe that this desire to set humanity free comes from Christ.

Yet it is pathetic and sad to see the attitude of many church leaders toward this monumental need. They seem to totally ignore the truth regarding this situation.

You understand that there are two truths. There is truth which might be called historic truth. It is real truth, but it is not relevant to spiritual life today. Then there is another kind of truth which might be called pertinent truth, that which is relevant to victory or defeat in our lives today.

It is this pertinent truth which I would like to present to you in these pages, because it is vital to your well-being and that of your loved ones. It is a truth which we must forcefully present and understand, because it is the truth which sets us free. (John 8:32.)

John 8:36 tells us that "if the Son sets you free, you will be free indeed" (NIV). When Jesus sets us free, we are free. When we know freedom, we can share freedom. God wants us to share that freedom.

It is amazing to me that the secular media today gives more attention to the subject of alien entities than does the modern Church. Recently, *Time Magazine* devoted a whole page to the story of a man named Charles in whom psychiatrists reportedly discovered twenty-seven different personalities. Ten years ago no great magazine would have published such a report, but today such stories receive national attention and coverage from the press and television.

It is also amazing to me that the Church of Jesus Christ hardly addresses such problems today. I believe that the Church has the answer to human problems. We must come out of the closet and make ourselves available to those in need. I further believe that no church has a right to expect support from the people if it cannot render to the people what they need.

Recently a person came to me requesting prayer for an emotional problem. I said, "Yes, I'll pray for you. What church do you belong to?" The person told me and I asked, "Did you talk to your pastor about this situation?"

"Oh, yes."

"And what did he do?"

"He recommended a psychiatrist."

The Church must cease being a referral station! It must stand up in God's Name and proclaim, "We've got the answer to *every* human need!'' We must believe that, and then start acting on it.

U. S. News & World Report noted that there are an estimated thirty-five million depressed people in this country today. Again, these aren't preachers being quoted, but psychologists and psychiatrists. When the medical profession of our country can recognize a problem, why haven't our ministers recognized it before?

There needs to be a dynamic awakening in the body of believers. This is one of the greatest needs which has ever confronted the Christian Church. When there are thirty-five million people living in the gloom and doom of depression in one land, they need to be brought out of it. Drugs may provide temporary relief, but they cannot deliver. We need Jesus Christ the Son of God to set people free.

I challenge every minister in our land, in Jesus' Name, to rise up and believe the Bible. Exercise your faith. Go and do the works of the Lord Jesus as you have been commanded to do. If you will, ours will be a different world.

Man's knowledge and experience in religion, science, technology, psychology, or philosophy is limited and deficient regarding the otherworld or ether world entities. Man has knowledge enough to go to the moon; but when a person loses his mind, man's knowledge fails. Modern man does not know what to do about an alien entity when it manifests itself in a human personality.

There are hundreds, perhaps thousands, of teachings on alien entities today. We have scores of books, magazines, and pamphlets at our disposal. Yet when this phenomenon occurs, man has no answer to it, no solution for it. He simply does not know what to do when confronted with alien manifestation. This is where you and I as Christians come in—not as scientists, but as disciples of the Lord Jesus Christ. We must be knowledgeable about these things. We must demonstrate to the world that there is an answer, and that we have the answer in the power and Name of the Lord Jesus Christ.

If the citizens of this world could somehow recognize and accept this truth, we could win the battle against ignorance. Nowhere is that ignorance more evident or more prevalent than in the modern Church.

The Modern Church Position

It is remarkable that the primitive people in the jungles of Africa or the high mountains of Tibet know more about alien entities, or demons, than most seminary professors and pastors of churches in so-called Christian countries. It is a pity that some primitive people know more about the spirit world than cultured Western world people. This means we must come to know and accept our God as a great and mighty God, Who can set humanity free.

Some religious leaders feel that as they have not personally experienced an encounter with an alien entity, such beings are not real.

According to the book of Revelation, there are seven church ages. The ultimate one is represented by the Laodicean Church. The Laodicean Church is the one to which the Lord says:

I know thy works, that thou art neither cold nor hot: I would thou wert cold or hot.

So then because thou art lukewarm, and neither cold nor hot, I will spue thee out of my mouth.

Revelation 3:15,16

In our modern Church today, we are living in the last church age, that of the Laodicean Church. What does our Laodicean Church propose to do about emotionally sick people?

Some will say that alien entities don't exist, that demons are the figment of a deranged mind.

The Bible says, **Now the Spirit speaketh expressly, that in the latter times some shall depart from the faith, giving heed to seducing spirits, and doctrines of devils** (1 Tim. 4:1). The Bible would not have said that there were devils (demons) if they did not really exist. Satan and his cohorts are very real, and they are your worst enemies.

Modern religion, on the other hand, teaches that if alien entities do exist, they are not so bad and that the Church should not be terribly concerned about the matter. God's Word, however, warns us in 1 Peter 5:8, **Be sober, be vigilant; because your adversary the devil, as a roaring lion, walketh about, seeking whom he may devour.**

Today's theologians in their referral of modern man's needs say that psychology, psychiatry or drugs can handle the problem of alien entities. One visit to a hospital for the mentally ill can tell you that this is just not true.

11

There are people who have been locked up in institutions for 30 or 40 years, being given strong medication or electric shock treatments for years, and they are no better off than they were at the beginning.

Another fallacy of modern theology is that to discuss the subject of demons would be to exalt Satan and his kingdom. This theory holds that the Church must be quiet and ignore the problem, then it will go away. Of course, this is not true at all.

If you evade an issue or problem, you will never find the solution to it. If you are not willing to be a valiant soldier of the cross, you're not going to win any victories. God is looking for people like Paul who are not afraid to recognize and confront the enemy, wherever he might be.

If you think our teaching on this subject exalts the devil, then the next time you see him, ask him! You'll discover that among all of those he doesn't like, my name is at the head of the list, because I have hurt him as much as or more than anybody else!

Satan hates the truth. He doesn't ever want who he is and what he is to be revealed. That's the reason he parades as an angel of light. (2 Cor. 11:14.)

Some modern theologians say that the subject of demons is relative, unimportant, and negative. Yet Jesus spoke more about demons than about angels. He talked more about hell than about heaven. Was He negative? Was Jeremiah negative? Was Isaiah negative? We must learn to face the truth and speak the truth— not just what people want to hear.

Some religious leaders say the subject is *relative*. It is not relative when millions of people are dying of it, being destroyed by it. It is not relative, and neither is it negative, to set people free. It's positive! You should see and hear the joy that comes into the lives of those set free from the powers of darkness, the thankfulness expressed to Almighty God for their deliverance.

The theologians of this Laodicean Church say from the pulpit, through books, by radio and television, that we should avoid the subject of demons because it is an immaterial or impossible situation.

We believe it is possible to cast out demons. If a person needs deliverance, we believe the Church has a responsibility. Christians are in a position to set people free. But in order to do that, we must first recognize that these entities exist, and that we have power and authority over them in the Name of Jesus. Then we must be taught how to use that authority and power.

The modern Church will teach you that it is better to "underbelieve" on this subject than to "overbelieve." They say it is better to be too quiet than noisy, to say nothing rather than to risk being labeled a "fanatic." Let me say that I would rather overbelieve than underbelieve any day! If there is going to be any point on which I am extravagant, it is on belief. It is an impossibility to "overbelieve" in Jesus. You cannot "overbelieve" in the power of God.

God is looking for people today who are dedicated to the truth, dedicated to the anointing, dedicated to God's power, dedicated to deliverance. God is looking for men and women to stand in the gap for our nation today.

I believe the greatest time in the history of the world for deliverance is upon us. I am so excited that it is time to set humanity free! We are not living in a dead age, but in a dramatic moment, a time when God is going to do more, and more.

Also some moderns teach that man does what he does without regard to temptation or alien entities, that he is what he is and nobody can do anything about it.

If a child is placed in an adverse environment, one in which he is exposed to sin and degradation, that child will be different from the one brought up in a truly godly home. It doesn't take much sense to know that. Look around you at our prisons and see those youngsters who are thrown in with hardened criminals. Or look into homes in which kids as young as six or seven are exposed to crime, incest, alcohol and drugs. Outside influences most certainly do have a bearing upon our lives.

The Alternative View

My travels in over 100 nations and ministering in all different kinds of cultures have brought me to a different determination from that of modern theology. Let me give you some examples from my own experience.

In the back country of Sao Paulo, Brazil, I was traveling by bus. At a small town the bus stopped to let off passengers. There in front of the bus station was a man tied to a pole. He was a mad man. He was like an angry animal, lunging at his tormentors and screaming obscenities. The man was large, almost naked, with long, unkempt hair. He was filthy from having lived in the dirt like an animal. The children threw things

14

at him, while the adults stood back and laughed. The people said he had no family. He was dangerous, they said, so they had tied him up as a public spectacle, much like the demoniac of Gadara in the Bible. (Luke 8:26-40.)

As our primitive bus bumped on down the red dirt road, I continued to relive that scene. That night as I preached, I could not forget that man! He was a human being and yet he was not. He possessed an immortal soul, but an alien entity now controlled him. He had a God-given right to be free and normal, but he had been reduced to the level of a wild animal.

Only the devil could find joy in such a sad situation. That sight of the mad man could happen in a thousand towns and villages in our present world. In spite of what religion seeks to teach in its inability to resolve the emotional needs of this generation, it is a confrontation like the mad man at the bus stop in Brazil, South America, that makes me say with Hebrews 13:8: **Jesus Christ the same yesterday, and to day, and for ever.**

One of the first persons I ever met who was possessed of an alien entity was a little old woman in Chicago. I had gone there to speak for the Christian Businessmen's Committee on their noon radio program.

As I stood by the door to leave the broadcast area, the little woman slipped up to me and cautiously said to me, "They are all against me here."

"Who?" I asked sympathetically.

"All of them," she replied with a sweep of her hand.

Who was this shriveled-up old lady referring to, I wondered. I knew those she pointed toward were fine Christian ladies and gentlemen. There was the celebrated minister, Dr. Oswald J. Smith of Toronto, for instance. He was one of the most compassionate people I had ever met. There were the local business executives who had paid for the broadcast and who loved souls. There was also the widow of the great evangelist Billy Sunday, one of the loveliest ladies you could ever imagine.

I said softly, "Why are they against you?"

In great fear she replied, "They hate me."

I said, "Oh no, they love you."

The little woman shook her head and moved cautiously down the street looking left and right to see if her imaginary enemies were pursuing her.

These great Christian leaders possibly didn't even know that this little old woman existed. But an evil spirit in her drove her along, talking to the spirit as she walked hurriedly, into a place of seclusion.

That was another person I couldn't get out of my system. I couldn't forget her! I said, "God, somebody has to deliver that woman."

You might ask, "Well, why didn't you do it?"

Because I had to grow up in this matter of casting out demons. I wasn't born with that knowledge and ability. I had to discover it, just as you do. I had to get disturbed inside before I could discover the truth about alien entities and about my power and authority over them as a Christian. Once I got disturbed inside,

God told me to go, take authority in His Name, and set humanity free. That is my ministry now. It is *your* ministry too—if you are a born-again, Spirit-filled believer. Our business as Christians is to set humanity free.

May your spirit reach out with Christ's Spirit to those crippled personalities seeking rest and finding none.

No Harm to You

In presenting alien entities from the divine and Biblical point of view, I can assure you that after more than 50 years of study and observation in more than 100 nations, you have absolutely nothing to fear in acquainting yourself with this subject. The Bible says in 1 John 4:4: **...greater is he that is in you, than he that is in the world. It also tells us in James 4:7: ...Resist the devil, and he will flee from you.**

Some would say that it is dangerous to talk about the devil. I disagree. I cannot see where discussing our enemy has any wrong associated with it, or any danger. The Lord Jesus told us more about the devil than any other person in the entire Bible. He renounced and denounced the devil more than any other recorded person. He gave strict orders to His apostles to cast out devils:

> **Then he called his twelve disciples together, and gave them power and authority over all devils, and to cure diseases.**
>
> **Luke 9:1**

> **And when he had called unto him his twelve disciples, he gave them power against unclean spirits,**

17

to cast them out, and to heal all manner of sickness and all manner of disease.

Matthew 10:1

The 70 disciples sent out by the Lord returned, rejoicing that they had power over devils:

And the seventy returned again with joy, saying, Lord, even the devils are subject unto us through thy name.

Luke 10:17

In the Great Commission of our Lord, He stated:

And these signs shall follow them that believe; In my name shall they cast out devils....

Mark 16:17

It appears that the less we say about the devil, the greater gains he makes in the world. He would like to silence those who would destroy him and his works.

There are people who, if you speak about the devil, accuse you of being *negative.* However, I am sure this is all part of the devil's strategy to keep people quiet about him. People in ignorance easily fall prey to the wiles of the devil. It is enlightened people who know how to stay free from his powers. In the darkened heathen lands he walks forth boldly to bind and destroy, and no one is able to stand up against him. In Christian lands we can speak like Paul who said in 2 Corinthians 2:11: **Lest Satan should get an advantage of us: for we are not ignorant of his devices.**

Satan quickly recognizes those who are able to control him. To the seven sons of Sceva who tried to cast him out without proper authority and power, he said: **...Jesus I know, and Paul I know; but who are ye?** (Acts 19:15).

I personally feel it is not discussion which is needed with the devil, but confrontation. Jesus Christ came to destroy his works and we are in the same business. Every day we should learn better how to destroy him. We do not discuss him in fear, but we speak of him in the light of the great victory achieved by the Lord Jesus Christ through His death and resurrection.

The world of psychology and psychiatry is baffled and awed over the worldwide plague of multiple personalities. The only answer is found in the Bible—the solution is spiritual and God-directed, not soulical and mind (psyche) directed.

Since authorities estimate that 35 million Americans need healing from depression, shall we go to the Bible with a deep desire to understand the complexity of the emotional human problems?

There is an answer!

2
What Are Alien Entities?

What are these alien beings which take it upon themselves to live in a human body? It is remarkable that the Bible says more about alien entities than it does about angels—heaven's ambassadors. There are more than 300 references to these alien entities in God's Word, some of them taking a page to describe. If heaven takes that much notice of them, then we had better take notice, too.

Are these alien entities real? In Revelation 12:7-9 we find these words:

> And there was war in heaven: Michael and his angels fought against the dragon; and the dragon fought and his angels.
>
> And prevailed not; neither was their place found any more in heaven.
>
> And the great dragon was cast out, that old serpent, called the Devil, and Satan, which deceiveth the whole world: he was cast out into the earth, and his angels were cast out with him.

In heaven there were three archangels. There was Michael, the archangel who cares for the military matters of God, the fighting angel. Gabriel was the telecommunication angel who carried messages. Whenever anyone in the Bible received a message from God, it was always Gabriel who brought it. Then there was Lucifer, who led the choir, praise, and worship in heaven. There were three mighty contingencies of angels, each of which could have numbered a hundred million, because heaven is so great.

The leader of this third group of angels, Lucifer (or Satan), led a rebellion against God. He and his followers were defeated and cast out of heaven. This explains the origin of alien entities and their entrance into this earthly realm.

The devil is alien to the earth. He doesn't belong here. The world is not his home, it doesn't belong to him. The Bible says that everything God made on this earth belongs to man. Satan is an intruder, not a resident. He has no right to be here, and we have no obligation to grant him entry. We are to cast him out, to send him back to the void of space, off the planet earth.

The Bible says that the devil, day and night, accuses us before God, just as he did in the book of Job. Verses 11 and 12 of Revelation 12 say:

> **And they overcame him by the blood of the Lamb, and by the word of their testimony; and they loved not their lives unto the death.**
>
> **Therefore rejoice, ye heavens, and ye that dwell in them. Woe to the inhabiters of the earth and of the sea! for the devil is come down unto you, having great wrath, because he knoweth that he hath but a short time.**

Paul writes in 1 Thessalonians 2:18: **Wherefore we would have come unto you, even I Paul, once and again; but Satan hindered us.** Evidently Paul believed that Satan was real, and that he worked to hinder God's people from accomplishing His will on earth.

Peter tells us: **Be sober, be vigilant; because your adversary the devil, as a roaring lion, walketh about,**

seeking whom he may devour (1 Pet. 5:8). With that amount of truth, we know how to come against our adversary, how to destroy him by the power of the Lord Jesus Christ.

Verse 9 of that same chapter says: **Whom resist steadfast in the faith....** There is the way to defeat Satan right there: **Resist him in the faith**—not with your brain, not with your brawn. You resist Satan in your faith, steadfastly.

Not only are alien entities real, but they have their own doctrines which they preach. One is that homosexuality is good. Another is that abortion, the murder of a million and a half innocent babies a year, is all right. There are many others. We don't believe one of them.

First Timothy 4:1 states: **Now the Spirit speaketh expressly, that in the latter times some shall depart from the faith, giving heed to seducing spirits, and doctrines of devils.**

Someday I would like to take the time to list all the false doctrines the devil teaches. It would be quite a revelation. The biggest lie the devil has ever created and foisted on to mankind is that God's Word is not true, that we should not believe it. Every doctrine of Satan is a corruption of divine truth.

Another fact about alien entities is that they wish to communicate with humans. In 1 Corinthians 10:20 the Apostle Paul wrote: **But I say, that the things which the Gentiles sacrifice, they sacrifice to devils, and not to God: and I would not that ye should have fellowship with devils.**

One time I visited a Buddhist temple in China. It was called the Temple of Ten Thousand Gods. What are these gods? I talked to the head priest there about them. In the center of the temple was a great Buddha, perhaps 20 to 30 feet high, made of bronze, very expensive. I called the priest over and through my interpreter asked, "What can this god do?" (Sometimes it is nice to be ignorant.)

The priest looked at me and said, "Right now, nothing."

I said, "Well, what do you keep it here for, if it can't do anything?"

He replied, "Do you see down in front? We bring in food, rice and vegetables, and then we bring in the candles. We light the candles and then I begin to pray. The god is off wandering around someplace. When I pray, he comes into the image here. Then he can do things. We have all kinds of testimonies of what he has done."

He showed me a hole in the back of the statue and said, "This is where the spirit of the idol goes in and out."

"That gets much simpler," I told him. "You don't need this big fat Buddha here at all. All you need is that spirit that comes and goes. He's the one that's doing it all. If you have that spirit, you don't need this statue, right?"

"Well, yes," he admitted. "That would be true."

"Well, take him down then," I said. "You told me that he couldn't do anything, that it's the spirit off in the mountains someplace that has to come back inside of him to do anything."

Paul said that which the Gentiles (the nations) sacrifice, they sacrifice to devils. This is a good example. These people weren't sacrificing to a bronze statue, but to *spirits*, alien entities which inhabited that idol.

Another time I was in the high mountains of Luzon where I had built a church for a tribe of people. A few of them had gotten saved, and I went up to dedicate the building. Right in the middle of the village was a tree without a single leaf on it. Every two or three inches, the trunk was bent. I've never seen such a crooked tree in the whole of the world. It was diabolically crooked. At its bottom was the place where the villagers worshipped.

They told me, "Our god is the god of the tree. Our god lives in that tree, and we come here to worship him."

I could walk there at three o'clock in the afternoon and ask them, "Where is your god?"

"Oh," they would say, "our god's not here right now. He's gone someplace. But when we bring out the sacrifice and light the candles and begin to pray, he comes. He's mighty powerful when he comes."

Paul says the things which the Gentiles sacrifice, they sacrifice to devils, and not to God. **And I would not that ye should have fellowship with devils** (1 Cor. 10:20). Then in verse 21 he warns: **Ye cannot drink the cup of the Lord, and the cup of devils: ye cannot be partakers of the Lord's table, and of the table of devils.**

An alien entity is a foreign spirit which comes to possess a human. It occupies no physical space in a human, yet controls many of the activities of such a person.

Alien entities are malign. They are basically evil, being Lucifer's agents. They destroy the normal functions of a human in society.

These alien entities are fallen angels from heaven, now called demons. Since they are under the leadership of Satan, their master, they hate God because of the loss of their positions in heaven. Not being able to reach God to do battle with Him, they seek to destroy God's creation. The chief object of their hatred is man.

An alien entity forever seeks a human body for a manifestation of his self-interest, which is to destroy the works of God. Therefore this subject is not a side issue. Christians must not be ignorant concerning the existence of these beings and their manner of operation.

One of the ways alien entities try to destroy the works of God is by causing sickness. They have this power. Two examples of sickness which can be caused by these beings are dumbness and blindness; however, there are a multitude of others.

> **As they went out, behold, they brought to him**
> (Jesus) **a dumb man possessed with a devil.**
>
> **Matthew 9:32**

Here we read where one of these entities had caused a sickness, a physical situation. He came upon a man and caused his tongue to be locked, so he couldn't speak. A devil did it. Then Jesus cast the demon out and set the man free.

In the same Gospel we read: **Then was brought unto him one possessed with a devil, blind, and dumb: and he healed him, insomuch that the blind and dumb both spake and saw** (Matt. 12:22). This man was made both blind and dumb by a demon. So it is possible for various kinds of sicknesses to be caused by alien entities.

The worst hurt, of course, is emotional sickness. When your mind is gone and you are no longer able to think properly, to resist properly, that is the worst thing that could happen. These beings can also come against your body, but you can resist their attacks against your body as well as against your mind, or your emotions.

In 2 Corinthians 11:14,15 Paul tells us:

> **And no marvel; for Satan himself is transformed into an angel of light.**
>
> **Therefore it is no great thing if his ministers** (his demon spirits) **also be transformed as the ministers of righteousness; whose end shall be according to their works.**

Alien entities war against the saints. That's their business. If Satan masquerades himself as an angel of light in order to deceive people, then you can expect his demons to try to pass themselves off as ministers of righteousness.

How then can you tell the difference between true and false angels? It is not really that difficult. Let me give you an example from my own experience.

One time I was in Java holding a meeting. As I walked into the church, a woman caught me by my coat. I couldn't get to the platform to speak because she was holding onto my coat. I really didn't know what to do, so I leaned down close to her.

She spoke to me in English and said, "You have a black angel in you, and I have a white angel in me." Then she giggled.

I dropped my briefcase to the floor, grabbed both sides of her head, and said, "You deceiving spirit, you are a liar. Come out of her!"

The Lord set her free immediately. She began to smile and her whole countenance changed. Later she told me that she had gone to a witch doctor fifteen years before and had been possessed ever since.

Alien entities do try to manifest themselves as angels. But they can easily be recognized for what they are. Imagine telling me that I have a black angel in me, and the devil has a white angel in him!

In Ephesians 6:11 Paul exhorts us: **Put on the whole armour of God, that ye may be able to stand against the wiles of the devil.** Let me say again—alien entities war against the saints.

If we don't put on the armor of God, how can we expect to be victorious in this life? A Christian cannot lead a loose life and still be able to overcome the cunning and deceit of the enemy. The devil is tricky. We must be on our guard against his wiles.

God says that if we will be faithful to Him, there is victory and power in the Name of our Lord Jesus Christ. In verse 16 of that same passage, Paul reminds us: **Above all, taking the shield of faith, wherewith ye shall be able to quench all the fiery darts of the wicked** (one).

Alien entities seek to sow discord in our homes, our churches, our society. Jesus said in Matthew 13:39: **The enemy that sowed them is the devil....** I have a policy that I will not quarrel with human beings.

Alien entities are accusers. They are accusers of God. First Corinthians 12:3 says: **Wherefore I give to you to understand, that no man speaking by the Spirit of God calleth Jesus accursed....** If any person accuses God of wrongdoing, that person cannot be speaking by God's Spirit. Such accusation can only come from one source, the accuser himself, Satan.

> **And the great dragon was cast out, that old serpent, called the Devil, and Satan, which deceiveth the whole world: he was cast out into the earth, and his angels were cast out with him.**
>
> **And I heard a loud voice saying in heaven, Now is come salvation, and strength, and the kingdom of our God, and the power of his Christ: for the accuser of our brethren is cast down, which accused them before our God day and night.**
>
> Revelation 12:9,10

As this passage points out, if these demons accuse God, they are certainly going to accuse us day and night. Many things people say about us come from the devil. That is why we must be careful how we speak about others. When you start accusing someone else, you might be letting the devil talk through your lips. It is better to leave other people alone and do only what God would have you to do. Leave the judging to Him. I don't have time in my life to speak against what anybody else is doing. It's none of my business. I just want to talk about what Jesus, the Lord, is doing, and what I'm going to help the Lord do.

Alien entities are subject to Christ, **Who is gone into heaven, and is on the right hand of God; angels and authorities and powers being made subject unto him** (1 Pet. 3:22).

Just as important, perhaps even more so, is the fact that alien entities are subject to discipleship.

> **And when he had called unto him his twelve disciples, he gave them power against unclean spirits, to cast them out, and to heal all manner of sickness and all manner of disease.**
>
> **Matthew 10:1**

> **Then he called his twelve disciples together, and gave them power and authority over all devils, and to cure diseases.**
>
> **Luke 9:1**

> **And they cast out many devils, and anointed with oil many that were sick, and healed them.**
>
> **Mark 6:13**

A Baptist missionary once told me on my telecast in Indianapolis: "We had a revival in Africa. I told the people to bring all their witchcraft items to me. We built a fire and burned them publicly. There were shrieks of terror coming from the fire as we destroyed their gods. They were defeated. We ordered them to go into the uninhabited places and get out of there."

On another occasion, a Baptist evangelist who appeared on our show said, "Brother Sumrall, I've read everything you've written on this subject. I want you to know something: I cast out devils." He began to tell me of the people he had prayed for and cast evil spirits out of. They were set free.

I am so thankful to God that He can set people free when His servants have the faith and courage to act on their authority and power over demons.

Once my son, Stephen, and I were on a plane flying out West. He sat down by a man who had a book pushing up out of his pocket. It was one of my books entitled *Demons: The Answer Book.* Stephen said to the man, "There's a book in your pocket, sir."

The man pulled it out saying, "Yes. Do you know Dr. Sumrall? I went to his classes in South Bend."

It seems that he was a minister of the Seventh Day Adventist church in Michigan. He said, "I have a brother in the state of Washington, and he's possessed of the devil. I'm going to read this book all the way out there, and I'm going to cast the devil out of him." That is what God wants each of us to do—read the Bible and cast out the devil wherever we find him!

All authorities and powers are subject to Christ. When we are in Christ, and when we are speaking for Christ, there is no power above us. What a wonderful thing it is that we have the authority and the power in God to cast out unclean spirits.

One time while in Wisconsin I was lecturing on this subject. When I had finished preaching, a man who was wearing a clerical collar came down the middle aisle. When he reached the front, I could see that he was crying.

I leaned over to him, not knowing what kind of clergyman he was. He said, "I am a Lutheran pastor. I have put two of my members in the insane asylum. After hearing you speak, I have decided to get them out."

I said, "Yes, sir. You can do it. God bless you for your decision to do so."

Then I added, "There is just one thing I would like to ask of you. Would you let me know about it, please?"

He answered, "I sure will," and he turned and left the building.

About a week or ten days later, my phone rang. The voice on the other end of the line said, "Dr. Sumrall, I am the Lutheran pastor."

"Yes, sir!" I replied. "What's happened?"

"I went to the insane asylum," he said. "I laid hands upon my members. I cast the devil out of them, and I brought them home. They're all right now!"

In ignorance and compassion, this man had put those people there; but in faith and anger, he took them out. The same man—same nose, hair, eyes, ears, same fingers—but the authority of faith within him made him alive by the Word of God.

I suppose the greatest curse of mankind is ignorance. If you don't know, you can't do. If you don't know how to build an automobile, you can't build one. If you don't know how to perform surgery, you can't be a surgeon. If you don't know how to cast out devils, you can't cast them out. I've never known of ignorant people casting out devils. Until people are trained in the Word of God and by the Holy Spirit of God, until people know the truth and know how to use that truth, they cannot go out and do this.

We do have the power and the authority to cast out demons. They are subject to us as members of the

Body of Christ. We need to learn to take hold of the power and authority that is ours in Christ and begin to use it.

One Hundred Million

We can change the world if we will simply get the Word of God in our hearts and believe it.

If there were only a few people needing help, I would not teach these truths so strongly. But God spoke to me on the mission field and told me to come home. He said the time would come when there would be one hundred million Americans who would need to be set free.

That is why I spend my time traveling all over this nation, teaching people, enlightening and inspiring them to go and set others free by the power of God.

Alien entities have many names. I think it would be good for us to look at some of them. In the Bible Satan is referred to as:

A. *Lucifer.* Isaiah 14:12.

B. *Devil.* Revelation 12:9.

C. *Beelzebub.* Matthew 10:25.

D. *Belial.* 2 Corinthians 6:15.

E. *Adversary.* 1 Peter 5:8.

F. *Dragon.* Revelation 12:3.

G. *Serpent.* 2 Corinthians 11:3.

H. *God of this world.* 2 Corinthians 4:4.

I. *Prince of this world.* John 12:31.

J. *Prince of the power of the air.* Ephesians 2:2.

K. *Wicked one.* Matthew 13:19.

When we understand some of these names, we understand something of the nature and character of our enemy. His names describe what he is and what he does to human beings. As we study them, we need to identify him. Unless you can identify your enemy, you will never win a battle. You need to know who you are fighting, and that you have power and authority over him.

Alien entities fear Christ: **And, behold, they cried out, saying, What have we to do with thee, Jesus, thou Son of God? art thou come hither to torment us before the time?** (Matt. 8:29). When you become aware of who you are in Christ and begin to make use of that power and authority, you will discover that these alien entities fear and hate you also.

It is sad to say that as you get deeper into the things of God, people will misunderstand you. They will mistrust you. They will call you names. At that point, you are going to have to be like Jesus and say, "I will accept it because I know that God has called me to set humanity free. And I am going to do it!"

3

The Origin of Alien Entities

How art thou fallen from heaven, O Lucifer, son of the morning! how art thou cut down to the ground, which didst weaken the nations!

Isaiah 14:12

The Bible is careful to explain the origin of alien entities. The Bible is the only verifiable source of truth relative to alien entities. If you seek information in other areas, you could possibly, and most likely will, come up with something other than absolute truth on this subject.

For example, you can go to the primitive and pagan areas of the world today. People there will tell you, "Yes, there are spirits. They live here and there." But they will never tell you the solid truth about them, because they don't know the truth. They can't even tell you where these spirit beings come from.

With the Word of God, you and I are given the exact truth about these entities: where they came from, what they are doing, and where they are going. To those who study God's Word, alien entities are known as the key to human tragedy. If we were to eliminate alien entities from meddling in human affairs, we could solve perhaps half of the problems in the world today. It is necessary to turn the divine spotlight of Bible truth on alien entities in order to understand our present world situation.

Alien entities were created as angels. In their department in heaven Lucifer was their leader. Lucifer is described as having perfection of beauty and wisdom. He was named the Son of the Morning. No other creature was given such a name. He was called the Anointed Cherub That Covereth. He was elevated to a special and privileged position before the throne of God. His very garments were made of precious stones, reflecting the blazing glory of the Trinity.

Then how did this glorious archangel become an alien entity?

The Bible is careful to inform us in Ezekiel 28:17: **Thine heart was lifted up because of thy beauty, thou hast corrupted thy wisdom by reason of thy brightness: I will cast thee to the ground, I will lay thee before kings, that they may behold thee.**

This means that pride was the cause of Lucifer's downfall. Pride came into the heart of an angel. An angel is not a corporeal being. You and I have corporeality—flesh and bone. Angels are spirits, with souls, but with no corporeality.

The sin of pride came into Lucifer's heart. By looking at himself rather than at the Most High God, he decided that his beauty and his greatness were within himself. He also decided that he could live any way he wanted without falling from grace. He became conceited and vain. He tried to elevate himself above God.

So Lucifer, the archangel, caused rebellion in heaven. He influenced one third of the angels to become subordinate to him, to battle the Almighty. As a result, he caused those angelic spirits to be removed from heaven and totally lose their beauty and goodness.

In Revelation 12:4 we read: **And his tail drew the third part of the stars of heaven, and did cast them to the earth: and the dragon stood before the woman which was ready to be delivered, for to devour her child as soon as it was born.**

God did not make the devil. God made an archangel; and this archangel, through his own will, made himself evil. God did not create evil, Satan did. People become evil because they want to be evil, because they have a will to do so.

God did not make the devil. He made an angel, who made *himself* evil. Then he was expelled from heaven because only holiness is allowed there. Only God-likeness can remain in God's presence. Only the Spirit of the Most High can reign there. There cannot be two spirits in charge, so the devil was demoted from his exalted position, along with a third of the heavenly host.

These alien entities fell down to the earth. The Bible relates that an alien entity was present in the Garden of Eden. We don't know how much time elapsed from the fall of Satan until his appearance in the Garden. We only know that he was there.

Satan came stalking through the gates of Eden with only one purpose in mind: to cause these people to suffer the same things he had suffered—to lose the favor of God, to lose the place God had provided for them, to lose their relationship with the Most High. And he succeeded.

Remember this, that is what the devil wants for you too. If he can, he will disappoint, discourage or depress you and cause you to lose your relationship with God. That has been his business for thousands of years now. So you must resist him. You have to speak to him and say, ''Satan, you're depressed, but I'm not! You're sad, but I'm not! You have fallen from grace, but not I! I am on good terms with the Most High God!'' Then keep it that way.

So, this is the beginning of a titanic struggle that has gone on for at least six millennia on the face of this earth. These alien entities and their final action will end at Gog and Magog. This will be just before they are forever confined and forever tormented in what the Bible calls the lake of fire. (We shall study this in a later chapter.)

> And when the thousand years are expired, Satan shall be loosed out of his prison,
>
> And shall go out to deceive the nations which are in the four quarters of the earth, Gog and Magog, to gather them together to battle: the number of whom is as the sand of the sea.
>
> And they went up on the breadth of the earth, and compassed the camp of the saints about, and the beloved city: and fire came down from God out of heaven, and devoured them.
>
> And the devil that deceived them was cast into the lake of fire and brimstone, where the beast and the false prophet are, and shall be tormented day and night for ever and ever.
>
> Revelation 20:7-10

This is after the millennial reign of Christ. Does this mean then that we Christians will be tempted again? No, we surely will not be. When this takes place, we will be reigning with Christ.

Then who are the nations mentioned here whom Satan will attempt to deceive? These will be those born during the one thousand years that Christ reigns on earth. You must remember that they will never have been tried to see if they want to serve God. They will have been under the divine spiritual dictatorship of Jesus. So the tempter will be set free for the last time so it can be said that he has tempted every man from Adam until eternity.

For a brief time he will be let out of the prison where he will have been confined for a thousand years. He will go out to try to deceive the nations. He will go throughout the four corners of the globe. He will deceive many. He will gather them together to do battle. He will encompass the camp of the saints (which is Jerusalem), where he will be defeated and cast into the lake of fire, along with the beast and the false prophet. There he, his demons, and all those who have followed him will be confined for eternity.

In considering the origin of alien entities, we must remember that there is one devil, but many demons. The devil is the prince of demons:

> **But when the Pharisees heard it, they said, This fellow doth not cast out devils, but by Beelzebub the prince of the devils.**
>
> **Matthew 12:24**

Demons as described in the Bible are the angelic host who decided to follow Lucifer, the archangel, in his insurrection against God. This was a celestial revolt. In Matthew 25:41 Jesus said of the wicked: **Then shall he say also unto them on the left hand, Depart from me, ye cursed, into everlasting fire, prepared for the devil and his angels.**

We must remember that God is a spirit, angels are spirits, and humans are spirits clothed with corporeality, or a body. These fallen angels live in a negative world and are angry with God and His creation. Therefore, we can only expect that their functioning will be much like Satan's. In fact, they will be carrying out his wishes, desires and commands. There are no "good" demon spirits. They are in complete subservience to their master, the devil.

Categories of Alien Entities

There are various categories of alien entities.

The Bible teaches that demons have degrees of strength and authority. Jesus, speaking of epilepsy, said: **...this kind goeth not out but by prayer and fasting** (Matt. 17:21). Here He was revealing that some demons are so strong that it takes the total surrender of the Christian in dedication and divine union with Christ to rebuke and loosen the evil spirit and exorcise it from the possessed person.

There are demons who rule over large areas as lords or leaders and governors in the evil spirit world.

For example, in Singapore, when Buddhists come to worship, *Pa*, the ruling god of that city, demands that they come first to his temple and worship him, burning incense, before they go to any other of the many temples to worship. This is common knowledge among the Buddhists of that area.

Another strong example is that of Calcutta, India, which is named after the female goddess *Cali*. She is the ruling dignitary of the spirit world in that area, and is respected as the supreme ruling spirit of Calcutta.

Of course, a demon is neither male nor female; it is only the manifestation that elects to be known as male or female.

In reference to the weakness or strength of demon spirits, I find that a deaf spirit is the weakest and the easiest to dislodge and bring forth from a person. Epilepsy is possibly the strongest to combat and hardest to cast out. There are legions of different kinds of spirits.

Where Do Alien Entities Live?

Demons principally live in the air above the earth because the devil is the prince of the power of the air: **Wherein in time past ye walked according to the course of this world, according to the prince of the power of the air, the spirit that now worketh in the children of disobedience** (Eph. 2:2).

It might be that they also have access to regions below the earth's surface. There are Scriptures which reveal that these spirits are brought out of deep waters, out of pits, and so forth.

It could be possible that the headquarters of the devil is on the moon. There is no Scripture for this, but we know that the moon has a tremendous effect upon our earth. If someone goes crazy, he is called a lunatic, meaning "moon-struck." Medical science has stated that patients in mental hospitals become very unstable at a certain period of the moon; they may be normal for 28 days, then suddenly become stark, raving mad. This is an area for further study.

Devils live in dry places and that is where Jesus sent them: **When the unclean spirit is gone out of a**

man, he walketh through dry places, seeking rest; and finding none, he saith, I will return unto my house whence I came out (Luke 11:24).

They also live in evil places, and places where crime and murders have been committed.

I went into France after World War II. Many people there told me that there were certain areas in which the sound of the tramping of military feet could still be heard at night. You could hear the beating of drums, the firing of cannons, the groaning and crying of the dead. Demons inhabit such places of tragedy.

Once I was staying in the home of a fine Christian gentleman in Denver, Colorado. It was a large house, and the guest room in which I slept was in a back portion of the house, away from the area where the man and his wife were sleeping.

One night about 2:00 a.m. I was awakened. There in the door I could see the silhouette of a woman. The room was dark, but I could plainly see her standing there. I could distinguish her features. She was fair of face, a Scandinavian type, with long blond hair and blue eyes. She was dressed in night clothes and was carrying a pistol in her hand.

I immediately knew what it was I was seeing, and what had caused it to appear. Someone had been killed in that room at some time in the past.

The next morning I confronted the owner of the house. "Sir," I said, "Someone was killed in this house."

"No."

"Oh, yes. Someone was killed in this house. I'm further telling you that you have had problems here."

We looked at each other. I said, "Go talk to some of the neighbors who have lived here a long time. Ask them what happened. I'm telling you, a woman died in this house."

The man went to the neighbors and asked them, "I just bought this big beautiful home a few months ago. Who lived there before me?"

The neighbors answered, "A Swedish doctor."

"Why did he move away?"

"His wife shot herself in the back room and she died."

That was the same room in which I had been sleeping. The man came back to the house, amazed.

When he asked, "How did you know that?" I replied, "I saw her there."

"What did she want?" he asked.

"The spirit of suicide is in this house."

Then the man broke down and told me the truth. He said, "The first time in my life that I ever thought of committing suicide was in this house. I had been told by that spirit four or five times that the best way out of this was to take my life."

Alien entities can live in places of tragedy.

A friend of mine in England had three daughters. He moved into another house, and one of the daughters lived in a certain room there. She hated it. She begged her father to let her move out of the room. She said, "Father, please let me move out of this room. I'm going to die here."

The father laughed at her, but she died. He put another one of his daughters in the room. After a few nights, she too pleaded with him, "Let me out of this room, Father. Please let me out of this room." But he was a hard-headed man. He refused. And she died.

Then the man came to Howard Carter and asked, "What in the world am I going to do?" Brother Carter answered, "Well, seeing as you have no power to do anything, you had better move out of the place. You only have one daughter left."

No doubt, a terrible tragedy had taken place in that room. The spirit of tragedy was dwelling there, and it destroyed those two lives.

Spirits can live in evil places, places where there has been crime committed. All kinds of entities are in jails, prisons and such places. Oppressive powers are in those places where terrible atrocities have been committed. The people who came to these places with those spirits left them there.

If you live in a house that seems unusual or oppressive, either rebuke the spirit in Jesus' name, or sell the house and move out.

The heathen have special cities of devils. They have special mountains where they say that the spirits live. Often they have rocks or trees which are spirit inhabited. They have a real understanding of these things—more so, many times, than people in Christian lands who refuse to study the subject. Some have refused to stand up to the problem of alien entities.

They refuse to have any understanding and comprehension of it. In dealing with a truth like this, every expose' that we can make of Lucifer, who is Satan, will weaken his kingdom.

That is my purpose in writing this book—to expose Satan so that his kingdom will be weakened. How is he weakened? Through knowledge. When you know him, you are no longer afraid of him. You know how to combat him, how to cast him out of your life situations.

When you are properly educated, knowing the truth, you are more than a match for Satan! The Lord wants us to know that. He wants us to realize that every victory of deliverance for any person anywhere weakens Satan's hold on this earth.

4

The Primary Abode
of Alien Entities

In speaking of the abode of alien entities, we must understand that there are three heavens.

Our earth is the First Heaven. Originally God made the earth like Eden, a magnificent garden.

Satan's kingdom is the Second Heaven. Here he reigns as the prince of the power of the air. The Apostle Paul mentions this fact in Ephesians 2:2: **Wherein in time past ye walked according to the course of this world, according to the prince of the power of the air....**

Christ further illuminated this truth in John 12:31: **Now is the judgment of this world: now shall the prince of this world be cast out. And in John 14:30: Hereafter I will not talk much with you: for the prince of this world cometh, and hath nothing in me.**

God's throne is the Third Heaven, as revealed in 2 Corinthians 12:1-4 in which Paul wrote:

> **It is not expedient for me doubtless to glory. I will come to visions and revelations of the Lord.**
>
> **I knew a man in Christ above fourteen years ago, (whether in the body, I cannot tell; or whether out of the body, I cannot tell: God knoweth;) such an one caught up to the third heaven.**

> **And I knew such a man, (whether in the body, or out of the body, I cannot tell: God knoweth;)**
>
> **How that he was caught up into paradise, and heard unspeakable words, which it is not lawful for a man to utter.**

In this lesson we are dealing exclusively with the Second Heaven. Here, alien entities control this area under their chief prince, Satan, and from which place they invade the planet earth.

These alien entities seek to control nations, and they have already gained control of some on the face of the earth today. They also control some cities, districts, or other areas. They seek to possess human beings through whom they can express their evil.

I have observed alien entities who reside in a house and make it their chief place of operation. I have also known of alien entities using a tree or a heathen temple or a rock where devotees come to communicate with them.

Howard Pittman Visits the Second Heaven

Howard Pittman, a Baptist lay preacher and a police officer for the Federal Government in New Orleans for 25 years, became very ill. His colon ruptured, and on August 7, 1979, he was declared legally dead.[1]

As Howard lay on the hospital bed, the devil came to him in sweet words saying: "Don't breath!" "Quit!" "It will all be over!" "Rest in peace at last!"

---

[1]Howard Pittman's book, *Placebo*, is available through Christian Center Bookstore, 530 E. Ireland Rd., South Bend, Indiana 46624.

Suddenly, Howard Pittman's human spirit said, *This is the devil. I must resist him.* He cried out, "No! I will live."

At that burst of determination and exercise of will power, Satan fled from him.

Also on this night of August 7, 1979, Howard Pittman saw, by his spirit, his guardian angel lift his soul and spirit out of his body. He was escorted by his guardian angel to the Second Heaven.

Howard remembers that he did not leave the hospital room to enter the Second Heaven, he passed a dimension wall. Only spirit can pass through that wall. A wall between dimensions is all that keeps us from seeing the total spirit world.

I have refused to allow the devil to manifest himself to me. A thousand times he has said that he would manifest himself, but I have always said, "You will not. I won't permit it." I will not permit him to move through the dimension wall.

Howard Pittman could see his body on the bed. His spirit and soul were in the Second Heaven (the air).

This world, he discovered, was the place or area where "principalities and powers of darkness" rule. Here he saw demons by unnumbered thousands, in many different forms. These entities had different colorings and shapes. Some had human forms. Others had animal forms, while others were part animal and part human, like some pagan deities.

At the lowest order, there were those with hideous and revolting forms, such as those terrible images we see worshipped by the heathen. Their priests have seen these spirits, drawn them, and made images of them in stone or metal. These people worship spirits which look exactly like the images you may have seen in pictures or in real life. When you see these horrible-looking images, you know that they are fallen spirits. They are so terrible looking because of the sins they have committed.

Howard said that his guardian angel informed him that he must pass through this Second Heaven to enter the Third Heaven where he could appear before God.

Only spirits can penetrate that world. You will not be able to penetrate it until you have a glorified body like Jesus had after His resurrection. Many times spiritists get into trouble by trying to penetrate that world, that Second Heaven. They have no legal right at this moment to enter it.

It is in this Second Heaven where Satan's throne is located. Only spirit penetrates it. Demons in that realm are very much aware of human activities and the protection of the Holy Spirit and the guardian angels who watch over humans.

This Second Heaven is the scene of cosmic wars, as we see in Daniel 10:12,13:

> **Then said he unto me, Fear not, Daniel: for from the first day that thou didst set thine heart to understand, and to chasten thyself before thy God, thy words were heard, and I am come for thy words.**
>
> **But the prince of the kingdom of Persia withstood me one and twenty days: but, lo, Michael, one of the chief princes, came to help me; and I remained there with the kings of Persia.**

Satan is the prince of the kingdom of Persia. Daniel was not talking here about a human being. He said that the angel was more than twenty days in a cosmic battle with Satan before he could come to bring God's answer to Daniel's prayer.

Your prayers are answered when you pray, but the devil immediately sets up a barrage of warfare against God and against the angels of God. It may take time to get your deliverance to you. This is why many people seem not to get their prayers answered. They give up on receiving their answer. They forfeit it, before it has had time to reach them.

There is something similar to a military chain-of-command among these alien entities. There is strong government and a military discipline of rank and order. Some entities carry titles such as prince. In Ephesians 6:12 we are told: **For we wrestle not against flesh and blood, but against principalities, against powers, against the rulers of the darkness of this world, against spiritual wickedness in high places.**

A principality is an area over which a prince rules. Every evil empire in this world has a particular prince presiding over it. The power of these notable ones ranges from a small area to a vast empire. A satanic prince is given a special assignment and authority to function in the name of Satan. He accomplishes a special job that Satan has given him to carry out.

Each entity can perform only one job. I have found this to be true all over the world. According to the Bible, there are no general practitioners among alien entities. Each spirit has his own area of expertise. A spirit of deafness cannot cause blindness. He can call for help from other spirits, but he himself is limited to only one particular work.

The strongest entities are the warring entities. Howard Pittman was told by his guardian angel about the entities of battle. They look like a human, except they are much larger. They are colored bronze and other demons are subject to them. They stand some eight feet tall and are rugged like giants. They war with such heavenly personages as Michael and Gabriel.

The second important group of alien entities, according to Howard Pittman, looks like ordinary human persons. They travel only in groups and are always in second place as to authority. Some of their names are greed, hate, lust, and strife. Greed is a chief among the group.

The third group of entities were half human and half animal. According to Howard Pittman, this group was responsible for directing witchcraft, spiritism, and all pagan activity. In the witchcraft area of demon spirits are the spirits of fear, suicide, self-destruction and some demons who are mimicking departed humans spirits and those who manifest themselves as ghosts.

The fourth group or order of demons look like known animals and unknown creatures; they are called murder, brutality, etc. Some of these look horrible. Howard Pittman remembers that they were frightening in their appearance.

In remembering his ordeal, Howard reports that he saw yet another group of alien entities, those who dealt in mysterious, special situations and cases. They had the power to cause epilepsy and insanity.

He witnessed some entities so terrible that they are now held in chains. The guardian angel indicated that they had gone beyond their limitations and their superior alien entities had chained them.

The Second Heaven Subject to the Third Heaven

All subversive forces of the Second Heaven are under restrictions of the Third Heaven. In Luke 22:31,32 we read a remarkable statement made by Jesus:

> **The Lord said, Simon, Simon, behold, Satan hath desired to have you, that he may sift you as wheat:**
>
> **But I have prayed for thee, that thy faith fail not: and when thou art converted, strengthen thy brethren.**

The born-again believer cannot be destroyed by any force or power in that Second Heaven of alien entities because **...greater is he that is in you, than he that is in the world** (1 John 4:4).

You need never fear that the alien entities of this Second Heaven can come into this physical world and hurt you. You are clothed with the blood of Jesus and the armor of God. There is absolute and complete security there. When the Lord said, **Neither shall any man pluck them out of my hand** (John 10:28), it was to this group of alien beings that He was referring. And they know it.

All believers in Christ are instructed: **Resist the devil, and he will flee from you** (James 4:7).

What a Victory!

What a Glory!

What a Life beyond this present world!

5

Can a Human
Have Multiple Entities?

**And his fame went throughout all Syria: and they
brought unto him all sick people that were taken with
divers diseases and torments, and those which were
possessed with devils, and those which were lunatick,
and those that had the palsy; and he healed them.**

Matthew 4:24

I always look closely at the words of the Bible. It
is significant to me that God uses the words *torments*
and *possession* differently. That means that a person can
be tormented without being possessed. A person can
have a nervous breakdown and not be possessed. A
person can be deeply hurt inside yet not come into a
state of possession.

Some people are tormented by demons, others are
completely possessed by demons.

Alien entities are not new. The Bible records them
from thousands of years ago. Secular history records
strange and peculiar people through the centuries.

One such person about whom I have read con-
siderably is Rasputin. He deceived the royal family of
Russia and was one of the factors which caused the
downfall of the czars. This evil person called himself
a holy man. He worked magic upon the royal family
of that nation.

There was also Adolf Hitler, a possessed man. God only knows how many and what kind of demons were inside him. It is reported that on occasions he would scream like an animal, and he hated like a devil. He was possessed!

There is an abundance of modern cases of alien possession.

The 27 Faces of Charles

For example, there is the case of Charles. *Time Magazine*[1] described a young man 29 years of age who was found wandering in a dazed condition on the shore of Daytona Beach, Florida. The ambulance paramedics considered him retarded so they took him to a local hospital. (I personally find that many possessed people display a behavior of retardation. The entity within them is usually trying to hide his identity.)

This man, who called himself Eric, astonished doctors by addressing them in two separate voices. One voice spoke as of a frightened child who had suffered abuse. Then his voice would change and he would speak to the doctors as an adult.

He was admitted to the hospital on February 9. In March hospital personnel witnessed his face twist into a violent snarl. He screamed an unearthly growl and cursed vehemently. The hospital psychologist, observing the patient, tells of recording over 200 occasions when the entities spoke through this man.

There were two Erics, the younger and the older. Then Mark began to speak through his mouth. There

---

[1]John Lee, "The 27 Faces of Charles," *Time Magazine*, 25 Oct. 1982, p. 70.

was Dwight; Jeffery, a blind mute; and Michael, an arrogant athlete. Then, a female entity named Tina began to manifest. Eric considered her a whore and railed on her. Later, Philip manifested and began contesting Eric's rights. Si interacted as a religious mystic.

In all, Eric revealed 27 different personalities. Three were female; one was a lesbian. The entities would fight each other. One, called T. K., was so furious he finally put Eric in the hospital.

The man is still under observation and the doctors are puzzled as to what caused such strange entities to manifest.

It is a well-documented fact that a human can definitely be possessed by "alien entities" which God never intended for His created man to be tormented by.

Man's Three Elements of Personality

The truth is God created man with three distinct elements of personality:

1. His spirit—his God-consciousness. This is his born-again nature, his renewed mind.

2. His soul—his academic personality made up of his mind, his emotions, and his will. This was changed in man when Adam rebelled against the Most High.

3. His body—his five senses. With these man relates to the earth world.

Man was created to be subject to the Most High, to have fellowship with his God. The question is: Can a human refuse relationship with God and know alien entities?

Can a Human Manifest Multiple Entities?

In identifying multiple personalities, several questions should be considered such as: Are these personalities human, related to human personality? Are they divine in nature, or are they demonic?

It should be remembered that all life in this universe is to be judged by its manifestations. Good produces good and evil produces evil.

Alien Entities' Attitude Toward Humans

In history there have been reported humans who act different at different times. Different voices emerge from their throats on various occasions. At one time it may be a masculine voice from a girl's throat. At another time, there may be a feminine voice from a man's throat.

Some people have testified and witnessed that these entities often torment their victims in various ways. They hit, scratch, and even throw the victim around. It is also testified to that they have power to make the victim into a new and often strange personality. The victim ceases to be himself or herself.

The Three Faces of Eve

One such victim you can read about today was a woman called Eve. Her story (though I don't recommend at all that you read it) is told in the book, *I'm Eve*,[2] which was later made into a movie entitled, "The Three Faces of Eve."

---

[2] *I am Eve* (New York: Doubleday, 1977).

Eve had 15 personalities to manifest in her. In the book, *I'm Eve*, by Chris Costner Sizemore and Elen Sain PiHillo, the entities are described: "There have been ten or twelve of them since I saw Dr. Thigpen," one of the entities reports through Eve's mouth, "but most of them have died or just went away. There are only three of us now." (You cannot believe a demon when he says something like this. There might be forty of them now.)

"Her voice was low and infinitely sad," record the authors, "as if she were speaking of dear, departed relatives."

These were Eve's three main faces or entities:

1. Chris Costner—Wild woman.

2. Chris White—Worried woman.

3. Jane—Free and independent, one who constantly gets into trouble.

Besides these, there were 12 other personalities which sometimes manifested themselves. I see no reason for producing either a book or a film about such alien possession.

The Five Entities in Marie

In the book, *Tell Me Who I Am Before I Die*,[3] by Christina Peters as told to Ted Schwarz, we read of the strange case of a young woman named Marie. Page 178 relates: "For many years Marie had fantasized

---

[3]*Tell Me Who I Am Before I Die* (New York: Rawson Associates, 1978), p. 178.

about spirits, the devil, witchcraft, and related matters. Some of this came from reading and seeing fantasy and science fiction stories. They provided a light escape from her troubles, just as did the nurse/romance stories she enjoyed.''

In the book, Marie tells of five personalities living inside of her:

1. **Marie** was a nurse and a mother. She was sensible and level-headed.

2. **Linda** manifested as an alcoholic. She was sex-oriented and on drugs. She often talked of suicide. The entity Linda was full of anger.

3. **Charlene** was the entity that went between these other spirits to soothe things over.

4. **Christina** was a little girl.

5. **Michael** was an angel of light.

This was the way Marie saw the entities. Often the spirits would lie about who and what they were.

Alien entities always drag their victims downhill into moral and spiritual degradation. This is the problem that we face today. There are literally hundreds of thousands of Americans who need deliverance from demonic power, and we Christians are the only ones who can provide that deliverance.

When you read a story or see a film in which someone exorcises a spirit, then dies as a result, that is a lie. Jesus did not die when He cast out devils. Neither did Paul, Peter, or anybody else. That lie is part of the devil's plan to keep us from exercising our power and authority to cast him out.

The Brazilian Witch Doctor

Another strange case of demon possession was that of a Brazilian witch doctor whom I knew personally. I met him in Brazil in the capital city of Brazilia. He worked in the office of the President. He was a very kind, intelligent person. To meet him, you would never know that he had been a witch doctor for forty years.

Arlindo Barbosa de Oliveira had been employed by the executive branch of the Brazilian government for many years, yet many alien entities were manifesting themselves in him. He was normal most of the time and very abnormal at other times. (See Chapter 6.)

The Woman From New Mexico

Mrs. Susie Carillo from the state of New Mexico journeyed to South Bend, Indiana, to our offices to ask for a prayer of exorcism. I have never witnessed a person more possessed. Susie had a serpent entity which rattled like a snake. You could hear it ten or fifteen feet away. Her tongue went quicker and faster than any human tongue I've ever seen. She knew when this entity arrived and manifested itself.

Speaking with a deep masculine voice, this entity claimed to have killed Susie's husband with its own hands. I asked Susie's daughter, who accompanied her, about her father. She said that he had been found dead in bed and had not been sick.

Mary Magdalene Had Seven Entities

A lady from the town of Magdala on the shores of the Sea of Galilee met Jesus, and He cast seven devils from her.

We shall give full attention to this piece of history in another lesson.

In this lesson we are only establishing the fact that netherworld personalities do cross the dimensional wall of spirit and body to manifest in human personalities.

The Demoniac of Gadara

In Mark 5, we read of the demoniac who had 2,000 to 5,000 entities. He was called Legion because of the Roman Army counting system which was used to total the number of entities in him.

The legal authorities had tried to bind him with chains to no avail:

> **Who had his dwelling among the tombs; and no man could bind him, no, not with chains.**
>
> **Because that he had been often bound with fetters and chains, and the chains had been plucked asunder by him, and the fetters broken in pieces: neither could any man tame him.**
>
> Mark 5:3,4

This man cut himself with sharp stones and watched the blood gush out: **And always, night and day, he was in the mountains, and in the tombs, crying, and cutting himself with stones** (v. 5).

He lived in the high mountains and in cemeteries, without clothes, screaming and cursing. This was the activity of "alien entities."

Boy Burned to Death

In our own city of South Bend, Indiana, a man and his wife came to me for counsel. They had just moved from Detroit, Michigan, where a group of teen-aged boys had taken their son to a kids' club which met in a little shanty house they had built. After seeing a special television show, the boys poured kerosene over the boy, struck a match to him, and burned him to death.

The parents could hardly stand to live, so great was their grief and incomprehension. Their big question was: "What motivated these 13- and 14-year-old boys to burn our son alive?"

I could only explain to them that there are three powers in the universe. There is God's power which is holy and divine. There is the devil's power which is ungodly and demonic. And there is a neutral power called man who is influenced either by the divine or by the demonic.

The parents looked at each other and exclaimed, "This must have been the work of alien entities." They were correct. In the words of our Lord Jesus: **The thief cometh not, but for to steal, and to kill, and to destroy: I am come that they might have life, and that they might have it more abundantly** (John 10:10).

John Wayne Gacy

In my book, *Unprovoked Murder, Insanity or Demon Possession,*[4] I present the case of John Wayne Gacy, who was convicted of murdering 33 people in Chicago. *Newsweek* reported that Gacy was babbling that a third power (alter ego) whom he called Jock committed the murders. He did not even remember the names of the 33 people he had slain.

---

[4](Tulsa: Harrison House, 1981), pp. 30-34.

The Girl from Oregon

Some time ago, a girl from Oregon visited us. Her father, who was a minister, came with her. This girl, who was about 19 or 20 years old, had a masculine voice which spoke to me and said, "Bow down and worship me, and I'll give you the world."

I said, "Satan, you've already said that, about two thousand years ago. You sure are late." Then I commanded that spirit to come out of the girl and to let her go free!

The list of such instances of demon possession today in our modern time could go on and on. You will notice that cases of demon possession are not just recognized by church people, but also by physicians, psychologists, and even the national news media.

Demon possession is real. It exists today, even in modern America.

This generation must decide between the living God of the Bible or Babylonian sorcery—between a netherworld knowledge of spirits inhabiting the human body or the Holy Spirit of God. In Exodus 22:18 we are instructed by God: **Thou shalt not suffer a witch to live.**

God wants man to have no relationship with alien entities, except to rebuke them and to send them back where they belong. We are to order them out by the blood of Jesus, on the authority of the Great Commission. They have to obey us, because He is God and we are His servants. We can all do it, not just one or two of us. As children of God, we *all* have authority and power over alien entities.

6

How Does a Human Receive an Alien Entity?

Be sober, be vigilant; because your adversary the devil, as a roaring lion, walketh about, seeking whom he may devour.

1 Peter 5:8

There are many ways a human can become possessed of an alien entity or spirit.

At Birth

There have been babies, especially in lands where the devil is worshipped, who are impregnated with alien entities from birth. On a number of occasions I have been asked to exorcise a spirit from a baby or a small child.

It is difficult to know the reason for this phenomenon. The Brazilian witch doctor, Arlindo Barbosa de Oliveira, was baptized to the devil some two weeks before he was born. His mother went to a powerful witch doctor and begged that a strong seance be organized. She went into a coma and the witch doctor opened her dress. Over her naked body he poured the hot blood of a chicken that he had sacrificed, making the sign of the cross on her stomach. He said, "Whatever is here I dedicate to the devil." From that moment, Arlindo was to be the servant of alien entities.

These spirits manifested themselves in Arlindo from the time he was a baby. He said that when he was three years old he could write drug prescriptions in Latin for the sick and that any pharmacist could read and fill these prescriptions. At that age the child was not even yet able to write his native Portuguese, but he could write Latin, a language he could not possibly have known.

Arlindo said that his younger brother, who was in the same room with him, fell ill. Arlindo went into a trance and saw two evil spirits. They growled at each other and attacked his brother, each struggling for possession of the boy. When Arlindo opened his eyes, his brother was dead. The demons had killed him.

At a Place of Pagan Worship

Very likely in the pagan world many people become involved with alien entities at places of heathen worship. At these temples they seek and search for the supernatural to change their lives. Alien entities frequent such places of worship.

I admonish all people to stay away from Satan worship of all kinds, because in these places Satan has rights that he has no other place.

> What say I then? that the idol is any thing, or that which is offered in sacrifice to idols is any thing?
>
> But I say, that the things which the Gentiles (nations) sacrifice, they sacrifice to devils, and not to God: and I would not that ye should have fellowship with devils.
>
> Ye cannot drink the cup of the Lord, and the cup of devils: ye cannot be partakers of the Lord's table, and of the table of devils.
>
> 1 Corinthians 10:19-21

In the Bible, we are told not to have fellowship with devils, not to go to places where they are, not to intermingle ourselves with them thinking we can do so without danger. Jesus didn't frequent such places or associate with such beings, and we must not do so either.

By Giving the Flesh Dominance

When a person gives alcohol its full measure of desire until he becomes an alcoholic, a spirit of alcoholism enters him.

When a person gives vent to anger and screams himself into insensitivity, it is an open door to possession.

When a person gives himself to illicit sex, a strong power comes upon him. He cannot resist this alien entity and becomes enslaved to immorality.

It is possible for gluttony, the desire for food, to become more important than eternal things and for the person to become possessed by gluttony:

> For many walk, of whom I have told you often, and now tell you even weeping, that they are the enemies of the cross of Christ:
>
> Whose end is destruction, whose God is their belly, and whose glory is in their shame, who mind earthly things.
>
> **Philippians 3:18,19**

In a church in which I spoke, a woman came forward for deliverance. A masculine type of spirit spoke out of her mouth saying that she had gone to an adult movie house and was watching immoral scenes on the screen. The unclean spirit was in that place, and it said that through enjoying naked men and women cavorting on the screen, she had given the alien entity the right to enter her and torment her sexually.

When I asked if this were true, she nodded in agreement and said, "I teach the young people's Sunday School class in this church; I just went to that place to see what it was all about."

I commanded the unclean spirit to loose her and leave. It did, and the woman became gloriously free.

When any person goes into the devil's territory, the alien entities have rights and privileges they do not otherwise have.

By Inheritance

When I work with a demon-possessed person, I immediately inquire into his past, his parents and grandparents. Most of the time I find the answer right there.

The Filipina girl, Clarita, who was possessed by demons and who became a sensation to the whole country, was the daughter of a spiritist who gave seances in the home and practiced witchcraft. It seemed natural for her to be controlled by the devil. (See Chapter 14.)

In Java we were in the home of a man who was possessed of seven spirits or alien entities. He knew them by name and he thought they were his servants, but in fact he was the slave.

This man's wife was a Christian and a member of a Full Gospel church. She told me: "My husband said he has caused people to get sick and die through the power of these demons he worships. They do all kinds of things for him. They will not let me in the same room with him at night. I cannot sleep with my own husband because of them. I have not slept with him for several years, because the demons throw me out of bed, physically.''

She took me into their room and opened the closet. She showed me a solid silver dagger. ''My husband burns incense to this silver dagger,'' she said. ''He calls these spirits by their names, and they come. He worships them and sends them out on missions for him.''

Why didn't I set that man free? Because he did not want to be delivered. He was proud of the fact that he had seven entities within him. He boasted of all they could do for him. At the dinner table he spoke up and said that he would give his spirits to his son at his death. The son seemed delighted and looked forward to being possessed.

As preachers have often begotten preachers into the ministry, so possession begets possession. It is true that inheritance can bring alien entities.

By Pagan Dancing

During the dances of pagan lands—as in the Macumba dance of Brazil, or the voodoo rituals of Haiti, or the Sardance of the Muslims, or the Thaipusam of the Hindus—alien entities can fill the atmosphere and enter the dancers.

I have personally seen people dance until they fall to the earth, choking and vomiting by demon power. They dance and cry out to the spirits for possession, and they are possessed.

By Wrong Meditation

The Bible tells about spiritual meditation. The prophet David spoke often about meditating in the Word. The Lord Jesus often went into a quiet place of seclusion to spend time in prayer and meditation.

The heathen use meditation as a means of seeking out alien entities. They have certain body postures they assume, open hands and an undirected or neutral mind. They repeat a certain word or phrase over and over, begging alien entities to come and dwell in them.

7

Where Did Jesus Discover Alien Entities?

Our Lord Jesus, when He walked this earth, encountered alien entities in many different places:

1. In the desolate wilderness:

> Then was Jesus led up of the Spirit into the wilderness to be tempted of the devil.
>
> Matthew 4:1

Jesus dealt with the devil in the wilderness. Satan spoke to Him. He took Him up to a high mountain to tempt Him into falling down and worshipping him. But Jesus rebuked the devil. He resisted Satan the same way you and I are to resist him, by quoting Scripture: **Get thee hence, Satan: for it is written, Thou shalt worship the Lord thy God; and him only shalt thou serve** (Matt. 4:10).

2. In the synagogues among the religious people:

> And in the synagogue there was a man, which had a spirit of an unclean devil, and cried out with a loud voice,
>
> Saying, Let us alone; what have we to do with thee, thou Jesus of Nazareth? art thou come to destroy us? I know thee who thou art; the Holy One of God.
>
> And Jesus rebuked him, saying, Hold thy peace, and come out of him. And when the devil had thrown

71

him in the midst, he came out of him, and hurt him
not.

Luke 4:33-35

Christ silenced the man and commanded the spirit
to come out of him. In anger, the spirit threw the man
violently, but Jesus would not let it hurt him. He was
forever loosed from that power.

In our churches today, we need the gift of the dis-
cerning of spirits. The pastor of a Full Gospel church
in one of our major denominations called me one time
and told me that there were three witches worshipping in his church and he hadn't even known it. One
of these witches had a son. The pastor had prayed for
the son, but he died. In revenge, the witch pronounced
a curse on the pastor's son. He became ill and was in
terrible condition, near death.

How could a witch feel at home to worship in a
Full Gospel church? I don't know. But I do know that
such a thing would not happen in any church of which
I were a pastor. I wouldn't allow it! Those witches
would either have to get saved, or get out!

3. In the graveyard:

And they arrived at the country of the Gadarenes,
which is over against Galilee.

And when he went forth to land, there met him
out of the city a certain man, which had devils long
time, and ware no clothes, neither abode in any
house, but in the tombs.

Luke 8:26,27

4. In public crowds:

And when they were come to the multitude, there
came to him a certain man, kneeling down to him,
and saying,

72

> Lord, have mercy on my son: for he is lunatick, and sore vexed: for ofttimes he falleth into the fire, and oft into the water.
>
> Matthew 7:14,15

In Acts 16:16-19 we read where the Apostle Paul encountered a girl with an alien entity. The girl attached herself to him and followed him for several days, until he got tired of it and cast it out in the Name of Jesus!

5. In every place He went:

> How God anointed Jesus of Nazareth with the Holy Ghost and with power: who went about doing good, and healing all that were oppressed of the devil; for God was with him.
>
> Acts 10:38

It is possible for alien entities to be in various kinds of places, under various kinds of conditions. In all kinds of places a person can receive an alien entity. But in all kinds of places, a person can also be relieved of an alien entity and be set free.

8

Alien Entities and Children

But when Jesus saw it, he was much displeased, and said unto them, Suffer the little children to come unto me, and forbid them not: for of such is the kingdom of God.

Mark 10:14

Train up a child in the way he should go: and when he is old, he will not depart from it.

Proverbs 22:6

Remember now thy Creator in the days of thy youth, while the evil days come not, nor the years draw nigh, when thou shalt say, I have no pleasure in them.

Ecclesiastes 12:1

In any home, the little children are the weakest point. They are the most vulnerable to an attack of Satan. We must keep them free.

There are 1¼ billion children under 14 years of age living today. Please notice that most books written and films produced related to alien entities involve children. With the film entitled *The Exorcist*, it was a young girl who was demon possessed. A similar film recently produced for television presented the story of a young boy who growled and fought because of alien possession.

Extra-terrestrial personalities have become a craze in our country. The recent popular motion picture

E. T. featured a being, supposedly from outer space, a creature with powers beyond the normal. His contact on earth was a boy. The two became close friends. The extra-terrestrial craze soon spread throughout the country with this film becoming one of the movie industry's all-time dollar makers.

U. S. News and World Report of December 20, 1982,[1] quotes Dr. Charles Browning, a California psychiatrist, as saying that he sees the appeal of *E. T.* as a symbol of people's subconscious "yearning for hope and strength during troubled times."

How is a little creature from outer space going to bring hope in troubled times? It is almost unbelievable to me that educated, cultured, modern Americans have allowed themselves to become subject to such a philosophy, especially when it is directed toward our youth. All we have tomorrow is our youth. They are our inheritance. It is they who will run the world of tomorrow, if Jesus tarries. How they are brought up, how they are trained and fortified will determine the kind of society our world will live in.

We must protect our youngsters. We must love our neighbor's children as we love our own. We must take steps to assure that they all grow up free from demonic influences. If we don't, we will never be able to see the mighty victories that God wants us to see in the world. If this generation of children grows up demon possessed, we will have problems on our hands such as we have never imagined.

---

[1] Jeannye Thornton, "Today's Toys—More than Just Child's Play," pp. 67,68.

With creatrues from outer space, such as this one, the devil is preparing the world to receive alien entities. That's the whole satanic purpose behind the production of such universally popular films—to prepare the world to recognize and receive alien entities.

There are only three areas of supernaturalism:

1. **For God** to move supernaturally.

2. **For man** to be moved by God supernaturally, as in the story of Samson from the Old Testament.

3. **For satanic forces** to break through the division wall of the Second Heaven into the First Heaven and to possess men through demon spirits.

These are the only three possible areas of supernaturalism. What about "little green men from outer space"? Where do they fit in? They belong in the third category. They certainly don't belong to God. Nor are they any kin to human beings. Since they are neither of God nor of man, they must be from the third supernatural realm.

God is opposed to all supernaturalism that does not originate from Him. Man either lends himself to God's supernaturalism, or he lends himself to Satan's. There are no other sources. Therefore, extra-terrestrial manifestations are dangerous. We need to know that. It is vitally important. That is why the Bible warns us against them:

1. Hallucinations

> And Moses and Aaron went in unto Pharaoh, and they did so as the Lord had commanded: and Aaron cast down his rod before Pharaoh, and before his servants, and it became a serpent.

77

> **Then Pharaoh also called the wise men and the sor-
> cerers: now the magicians of Egypt, they also did in
> like manner with their enchantments.**
>
> **Exodus 7:10,11**

Moses was a man who had the power of God. Whatever he did was of God, for God, and for the people. These men who called themselves sorcerers, magicians and wise men were evil men. They had given themselves over to satanic operations. Moses had loaned his spirit to the right with God's power. They had given their spirits to the left, to the devil's power.

The human stands in the middle between two supernatural forces. He can have supernatural power, but when he does, it has come from one of two sources. He has leaned toward God for it, or he has leaned toward the devil for it. There are no other possible sources of supernatural power. If it is not of God, it is of the devil.

2. Impersonations

> **Regard not them that have familiar spirits, neither
> seek after wizards, to be defiled by them: I am the
> LORD your God.**
>
> **Leviticus 19:31**

As Christians we are to have nothing to do with familiar spirits, wizards or anything of that nature. We are not to seek after someone to tell us our fortune or someone to use supernatural power to find out things we do not know. We are to look only to God as our source of supernatural power and direction.

When you become associated with alien entities, you are no longer a clean person, spiritually. You have come under a demonic defilement. Only God can wash that away and cleanse you. That is what the Lord Jesus wants to do today.

3. Manifestations

And he doeth great wonders, so that he maketh fire come down from heaven on the earth in the sight of men.

Revelation 13:13

This passage in Revelation refers to the Antichrist system and the False Prophet, the evil one whose job it is to call and beckon people to the Antichrist.

There are many people who immediately regard any supernatural manifestation or wonder as coming from God and evidence of God. That is not necessarily true. As we have seen, there are three possible supernatural dimensions: God; man motivated by a power not his own; and Satan. If anyone claims divinity by doing wonders, the first thing you should do is to check on his morals. What kind of life does he lead? Get to know something about him.

The National Spiritualists Association is preparing what they call satellite seances. They claim they shall do exploits and other sorcery phenomena. The leaders have stated, ''The central issue will be contact with man's immortal spirit that relates to man's afterlife.'' They expect nationwide seances to be held to seek to contact the dead and to answer questions regarding the hereafter. These are to be broadcast throughout the world via satellite. They will find millions of our children sitting on the floor watching. In Jesus' Name, please be careful what your children watch!

Children Are a Prime Target

If some parents would get up on Saturday morning and see the television programs their children are watching, they would be shocked. One cartoon portrays the earth destroyed by quakes and floods. The civilization of men has been destroyed and replaced by a new civilization of black magic spirits called elves. This is an example of what our children are taught that the world of the future will be like.

Children are a prime target for alien entities. Many people tell me that their first manifestations of evil took place in their juvenile years. I have prayed for more children than adults. Jesus delivered at least four children that we know about:

1. **The epileptic boy,** healed of seizures. (Mark 9:17-37.)

2. **Jairus' daughter,** raised from the dead. (Luke 8:41,42,49-56.)

3. **The widow's son,** raised from the dead. (Luke 7:12-15.)

4. **The daughter of the woman from Sidon,** delivered from demon possession. (Matt. 15:21-28.)

Jesus raised the widow's son from the dead because of His compassion for her, but the other three were restored because of the persistence of their parents.

It was a damsel, a girl who was being used as a fortune teller, out of whom Paul cast the spirit of divination in Acts 16:16-18.

Cornelio, the invisible boy about whom we will study in Chapter 14, was only about 12 years old.

Clarita, the girl who was delivered from demon possesion in a Philippine jail, was 17.

The Brazilian witch doctor was only three when he began to write prescriptions under the power of an alien force.

There are many, many others I could name, such as the girl in California who tore up her family's house, and the deaf and dumb boy I prayed for and delivered in the city of Taytay, in the Philippines.

Extra-terrestrial Consciousness

An extra-terrestrial consciousness can be produced in several ways.

One way is by a drug state of an altered conscience. Of all prescriptions that were filled last year, over 50 million of them were for hallucinogenic drugs.

It can be produced by an alcoholic state. Over 10 million Americans are now declared alcoholics. They live in the unreal world of an altered state of mind. It is a world that brings sorrow, destruction and death.

There is transcendental meditation. The TM teachers, or gurus, make varied claims of releasing and expanding the human mind through the transcendental meditation. They make claims of higher conscience attainments which can bring self-fulfillment and self-expression.

To get meditation people into the world of the extra-terrestrial, the guru introduces a Hindi phrase of worship called the *mantra*. The *mantra* is only one or two words. It is a secret formula from the Hindi language spoken during meditation. If the *mantra* is spoken fast enough and long enough, it is said that it will control the subconscious mind. What the meditator does not know is that the *mantra* are sounds and code words of praise or pleading with Hindu deities. The Bible is careful to explain that such worship is a worship of devils and not of God.

Extra-terrestrial consciousness can be very dangerous for the human. It can break his relationship with the true and living God. The first of The Ten Commandments given to us is: **Thou shalt have no other gods before me** (Ex. 20:3).

King Saul Knew the Extra-Terrestrial World

King Saul, the first king of Israel, sold himself to alien entities and became possessed of the devil:

> **Then said Saul unto his servants, Seek me a woman that hath a familiar spirit, that I may go to her, and enquire of her. And his servants said to him, Behold, there is a woman that hath a familiar spirit at Endor.**
>
> 1 Samuel 28:7

> **But the Spirit of the LORD departed from Saul, and an evil spirit from the LORD troubled him.**
>
> 1 Samuel 16:14

> **Then said Saul unto his armourbearer, Draw thy sword, and thrust me through therewith; lest these uncircumcised come and thrust me through, and abuse me. But his armourbearer would not; for he was sore afraid. Therefore Saul took a sword, and fell upon it.**
>
> 1 Samuel 31:4

We Must Bring Our Children to Jesus

> And, behold, a woman of Canaan came out of the same coasts, and cried unto him, saying, Have mercy on me, O Lord, thou son of David; my daughter is grievously vexed with a devil.
>
> Matthew 15:22

> And Jesus rebuked the devil; and he departed out of him: and the child was cured from that very hour.
>
> Matthew 17:18

> But when Jesus saw it, he was much displeased, and said unto them, Suffer the little children to come unto me, and forbid them not: for of such is the kingdom of God.
>
> Mark 10:14

In Houston, Texas, a ten-year-old boy cursed his father and told him to leave home. The father was a medical doctor, yet he had no power to heal his own son.

In Atlanta, Georgia, a boy five years old chewed his tongue and banged his head constantly. But his father would not come with him for prayer.

The bodies of children belong to their parents. They must agree together and they must seek God together. We must bring our children to Jesus for healing and protection from demonic possession.

Demon possession is a very real thing. If you haven't known of these kinds of situations, there is no doubt that before long you are going to discover children who are hurt by the power of the devil. God wants you and me to set them free by His mighty power.

9

Alien Entities and Crime

The thief cometh not, but for to steal, and to kill, and to destroy: I am come that they might have life, and that they might have it more abundantly.

John 10:10

The thief of whom Jesus is speaking here is the devil. He comes for three reasons:

1. To steal.

Any good thing that you have, the devil wants to take from you. If you have a good family, home, job, business, or health, Satan comes to try to steal it away from you.

2. To kill.

Not only does Satan come to steal, he also comes to kill any good thing that he can find or touch.

3. To destroy.

Satan wants to annihilate good, to sweep it away until nothing is left of it.

By contrast, Jesus came to give you life, life in all its abundance. That's the only kind of life God wants you to have. He doesn't want you to have a portion, or a half measure. He wants you to have abundant life. Abundant means overflowing, more than you need, so you can share with others. God is the giver of abundant life. He wants us to have that abundant life.

I have a feeling that many times we resist the temptation when we should be resisting the tempter. We say to the temptation, "Go away." Then we let the tempter bring it back again. We need to resist the tempter more than the temptation.

Temptation should be avoided, but the tempter is the one who brought it. So our fight is not against temptation, but against the one who does the tempting. We need to learn to move him back from us so we can walk freely in the Lord Jesus and enjoy the abundant life He came to give us.

In most cases, alien entities are not particularly crime related. This means that possessed people hurt themselves more than others.

However, there are destructive spirits and killer spirits. In our nation of 225 million people, there are over 20,000 murders annually. That means that in America, every 24 minutes someone is murdered.

One half of all murdered people are killed with a weapon other than a gun and 30% of all homicides are unsolved. In New York City 43% of all murders go unsolved.

Thousands of senseless murders are committed every day. There are those who live in terrorized communities. They live in dread of death.

Multiple and unprovoked murder is a sign of alien activity.

I have given my book on the subject of unprovoked murder to judges who have ruled that a murderer was not guilty on the grounds of temporary insanity. In this book, I show how the murderer's "insanity" has nothing to do with his ability to drive a car, conduct his business, or carry out his daily routine of activities.

I say to those involved in the judicial process: "You are mistaken. This man is not insane. He is perfectly capable of taking care of himself. He is normal in every way, except that he killed someone. Why? What possessed such a person to do such a thing?" Then I tell them what "possessed" him—an evil spirit that cries out for blood!

Usually these people do not want to accept that answer. But I can assure you of one thing: If it keeps happening, they will learn to accept it.

For example, in the Richard Benjamin Speck case, the spirit of murder in him demanded the blood of innocent nurses in Chicago. He had never met them and had no reason for brutally murdering them. Yet he slipped into their dormitory, took a knife, and cut them up as if he were cutting up beef. He killed them, then scattered their blood and pieces of their bodies all over the place.

One time I preached in Washington, D.C., at a Full Gospel Businessmen's banquet. I preached about the forces of demon power in our world today. When I had finished speaking, a high-ranking F.B.I. official came up, took me by the hand, and said, "You are the first man I've ever heard speak who told the truth about crime. It isn't prison these people need. They need the devil cast out of them."

Then he went on to say, "There is something in these people that causes them to do what they do. You can put them in prison as long as you want to, but it doesn't change them. Sometimes, even in prison, they kill there also."

We believe that alien entities cause crime. We have evidence of it in some instances. For example, there is the case of David Berkowitz, called the Son of Sam. He sought beautiful girls to destroy them. He would kill these strangers for no apparent reason. This man, who said his dog told him what to do, was demon possessed.

A strong Church in the world could take care of problems like that. It could cause lives to be changed by God's power.

But I must be honest with you. Most pastors today would not dare say what you have already read in this book. Most ministers have no knowledge of demons or demon possession.

I can never forget being in classes in the University of Chicago. In my speech class there were Roman Catholic priests, Jewish rabbis, a couple of Episcopalian priests, and a Lutheran minister. All were about to receive their doctorates. As I got to know this group of men during that school year, I discovered that not one of them knew anything about salvation.

As part of our course assignment, each student had to deliver a prepared speech before the class. When it came my turn, I spoke about Jesus Christ. I told how He said, "I am the way, the truth, and the life." Afterwards the rest of the class was supposed to criticize my speech, to try to tear apart what I had said. These men did not know where or how to begin. They didn't know enough to discuss it.

"What kind of way was He?" one of them asked. "What kind of truth?"

"Total," I answered.

After class, as they stood around smoking their pipes, they confided in me: "We're scared. We're going to have to leave here in a few months and go out into the world. We're going to have to be pastors, and we don't know what to say or do."

I led those men to an experience in God. I showed them that there was human need and sorrow out in that world to which they were going. I told them they had to recognize that fact and go forth to care for those people in need. They had not been taught how to do that in the university.

If they did not know how to be saved, how could they possibly know how to help a person under the influence of the devil? Their answer to that problem was simple: have the person committed to an insane asylum. But that is not where the demon-possessed need to be. They need to be set free and sent back to their families.

In the Charles Manson case, five women lived in a strange hypnotic state around him. They treated him like a king. They often served him food and drink while naked, offering him anything his heart desired. At his command they killed actress Sharon Tate and the others. They could not have been normal. This had to be the activity of alien entities.

The Jim Jones case in Guyana could possibly be the strangest story of death ever known. Jim Jones boasted that he slept with many of the women who joined the group and denied their husbands the privilege of touching them. He led these people to a grisly death by suicide. This too had to be the work of demon forces.

John Wayne Gacy was charged with the murders of 33 boys and men in Chicago. He even slept with those he had murdered. The N.G.R.I. defense (Not Guilty by Reason of Insanity) is not true. These murders were the work of alien entities.

There are spirits that move against people to cause them to destroy others. Such activity is not human. It is unlike a man to commit such atrocities. To anyone with any understanding at all, it is evident that there is another power at work here. It is an alien entity that is functioning in such people as these. Inside they are crying out for life.

The devil hates life. He is the destroyer of life. Realizing that, it is then no wonder he gets into a person with the intention of destroying.

The Devil Can Possess a Human

The devil is real. He is evil. And he has the potential to possess a person's mental faculties and emotions.

A human *can* come under the power of an alien entity, a spirit that does not belong on this earth. It is alien to this planet and has no place here. Yet if received by humans, it can hurt them.

The Importance of the Human Mind

Within the realm of the human soul, possibly the most powerful element is the mind. The mind is capable of moving in any direction to learn and to train itself. There is no limit to the knowledge that can be accumulated through the facets of the human mind. Without a doubt, the mind is the most outstanding factor in the human personality.

With our mind we make decisions. These decisions make us whatever we are. The Lord Jesus said specifically that man should serve God with his mind:

> **And he answering said, Thou shalt love the Lord thy God with all thy heart, and with all thy soul, and with all thy strength, and with all thy mind; and thy neighbour as thyself.**
>
> **Luke 10:27**

Notice that we are commanded to *love* God with all our faculties. When we have love, it is impossible for alien entities to have any relationship with us. You would be amazed at the power of love. With the love of God in our hearts, when we are flowing in the love of God, alien entities cannot find a resting place within us.

There is security in the dynamic love of God. God's love in your heart can identify these entities and throw them out.

God's love is such a strength and such a power. But it is with your mind that you make these decisions. It is with your mind that you say, "I will serve God," or, "I will give my mind over to an alien entity."

The devil cannot take your mind from you. You must give it away.

Your will power is part of the trinity of your soul. In it, God gave you an independent will. He will not override your will, and the devil cannot.

I have talked with many people who were delivered from the power of the devil. All of them said that even when they were possessed, they did not always obey the devil. They still had a will of their own; they could do whatever they pleased. Every human has that will. We must have a will to resist Satan.

One beautiful thing you need to know. There is not one place in the Bible where God says you should be afraid of an alien entity. The Bible says to resist the devil and he will flee from you. Do you know what the word *flee* means? It means to run away in fear, in stark terror.

So you have nothing to fear from alien entities. If you had fear, how could you deliver other people? You have nothing to fear, but you do have to make a choice.

Every human mind on the face of the earth serves some entity, whether it be good or evil, whether it be God or the devil. With your rational mind, you make the decision to serve the Almighty God. You can think about God, calculating His greatness and His majesty, recognizing Him and honoring Him as the Creator of the stars and the seas and the mountains. Just as the human mind can be directed in its positive relationships, it also can be directed in its negative relationships. **You must choose!**

The Devil is Real

Every person must come to know that there is an entity of evil commonly known as "the devil." As long as a person or society denies this fact, it will be impossible for them to understand what really happens to thousands of human beings—not just those found to be criminals, but others who are intensely jealous or who go crazy with anger. This is not the result of God's power or human power. It is only one power: satanic power. The devil is real!

The Devil is Evil

Once we recognize that there is an entity in existence called Satan or the devil, then it is necessary to identify him. This is very simple: Satan is the source of evil, of all that is bad and ungodly. The devil hates God, he is angry at God.

There is a war going on between the forces of good and evil. It began when an archangel named Lucifer (or Satan) was dethroned. It will continue until Jesus Christ returns to earth, redeems the earth from Satan's power, and throws Satan into the lake of fire for eternity. Until then, the devil will strike out at God the best way he knows how, and that is by trying to hurt the objects of God's love: you and me.

Crime and sin are ways the devil has of mocking God. It is remarkable to me how people in Africa and Asia can worship the devil as they do. They worship an entity that shows absolutely no regard for them. The devil has no regard for those who serve him. Only God loves the people who serve Him as their provider. Until people realize this, they will continue to wander in a labyrinth of confusion in the world.

10
Is Witchcraft
an Alien Entity?

Beloved, believe not every spirit, but try the spirits whether they are of God: because many false prophets are gone out into the world.

1 John 4:1

I don't normally make this confession, but I have suffered more as a result of teaching what you are reading right now than for anything else in my entire life.

I grew up in a fundamentalist church which never taught about the devil. They made fun of him. They called him "Slewfoot' and made rather light of the whole matter of demonic activity. I have since discovered that when you do that, you cancel our your right to hurt him. The devil doesn't have to obey you if you ridicule him.

Satan is a prince. He is a power that must be reckoned with. In the little book of Jude we read where Michael and Satan were contesting with each other over the body of Moses. The Bible points out that though Michael was an archangel, he **durst not bring against him a railing accusation, but said, The Lord rebuke thee** (Jude 9).

I don't appreciate people trying to tell funny stories or jokes about the devil. I don't appreciate their saying that he has two horns and a tail. He is an angel of light and so deceptive that it takes a spiritual person to be able to recognize where and when he is functioning.

When I went to the mission field, to the Orient, beginning in Indonesia then on to Hong Kong, the Philippines, into Vietnam, then back into Southwest China, I began to encounter people who were completely abnormal. they would distrub our meetings. when this happened, something would rise up in me and command, "You come out of that person!"

I would see them instantly set free by God's power. After all, I couldn't have my meetings disturbed and broken up. If I did that, I might as well have stayed home.

So through persevering and reaching out to set people free, this ministry fell upon me. Because I learned so much about it in so many nations of the world, people have wanted to call me an exorcist. I have never sought that title. I didn't want it. Some people are almost afraid of me, just because I command unclean spirits to come out of people. I do that for the simple reason that God told me to do it. God told me: "You must teach others how to set people free. They will never see the jungles of Indonesia that you have gone through. Or the little villages high in the steaming hills of Java. Neither will they see those rustic villages in the top of Tibet. But you are going to have to help them know that they can set people free right where they are.'

So actually I minister not of my own will, but because God wills it. Frankly, I would rather just share some nice "gentle Jesus' stories. That way I would offend no one and we could both be happy. But if I just did that, what would happen when you came up against the Evil One and didn't know how to handle the situation? You would possibly be defeated in your Christian experience. I am sharing all this with you so you will know that the devil is real. He is evil. He is out to destroy your life. But there is an answer: the Lord Jesus Christ.

Unfortunately, there are many people, even some Christians, who don't know this yet. They get all involved in witchcraft, thinking it is a harmless pastime, or even something good. There are people in high places in this country who play around with witchcraft, with crystal balls, fortune telling, seances and many other such things, without really understanding what it is they are involving themselves in.

What is Witchcraft?

Witchcraft is defined as knowledge beyond normal human understanding. It deals with information which is concealed from view of the average human. Witchcraft is secretive and flourishes on that which is mysterious.

There are only two sources of power which can reveal hidden information or knowledge of a spiritual nature. One of these is God as described in the Bible. The other is Satan or the devil who constantly works in opposition to God.

When a person is experiencing a spiritual vacuum, he will normally seek one of these two powers to guide him.

Therefore, witchcraft is primarily religious in nature. Some seek to discover themselves through witchcraft and to fill a void in their lives. Some seek to communicate with their dead loved ones. Some seek to discover God through witchcraft. However, God can only be found in the Lord Jesus Christ:

> **Jesus saith unto him, I am the way, the truth, and the life: no man cometh unto the Father, but by me.**
>
> **John 14:6**

Until you find Jesus, you cannot find the Father. No one can come to God, but by Jesus. He said: **I am the door: by me if any man enter in, he shall be saved...** (John 10:9). Jesus Christ is the door to heaven, the door to God, the door to spiritual knowledge; and we can only come through that means.

God's Warnings

A Christian should never seek supernatural guidance through any other means than the Bible or prayer in the Name of the Lord Jesus. If the searcher for spiritual guidance goes to the netherworld of witchcraft for assistance, he separates himself from God and His holiness.

> **And when they shall say unto you, Seek unto them that have familiar spirits, and unto wizards that peep, and that mutter: should not a people seek unto their God? for the living to the dead?**
>
> **Isaiah 8:19**

This truth of separation from God is what America does not understand at this moment. That's your business and mine, to warn people that when they go to an alien source for spiritual information, they are alienating themselves from the one true God.

The Bible says that bitter waters and sweet waters cannot come out of the same fountain. Paul said that we must not have fellowship with devils. If a person wants to know something about life, he doesn't have to ask the dead about it. Why should he? What do the dead know about life? Absolutely nothing.

God says in His Word that if we want to know about life, we should come to Him, Who is the Author of life. He warns us about playing around with the things of the devil.

Witchcraft Hides Its True Identity

Witchcraft seeks to hide behind the door of the powers of darkness. When people have discovered to their horror and dismay that Satan is the source of their information and that his guidance is demonic, they often become depressed and sometimes filled with fear.

One of the young ladies of our church was in a Full Gospel Bible school. She and some of the other girls had gotten a Ouija board. They were having a rare old time with it. At night they would talk to the Ouija board and ask it questions: "Who am I going to marry? How tall will he be? What color will his hair be? What kind of eyes will he have? Will we get along well together?" They were having a great time talking to the Ouija board.

Finally, one of them said, "Let's talk to the Ouija board and ask him who it is."

So they asked the board, "Who is this who is talking to us?"

The answer came back, "Satan."

That room became so full of evil the young girl grabbed her telephone. She called her mother, a member of my church, and said, ''Pray for us quick. Our room here is full of the devil.''

Dabbling in the occult is dangerous. It can lead to all kinds of problems, including demon possession. Sometimes people spend five years getting into demonic activity, and then expect a preacher to get them out in five minutes. Sometimes it takes a cleansing period before people can be totally restored, time to get inside the person and make readjustments, time to get things right with God again.

Witchcraft Banned

God forbids any occult activity by His people and all forms of witchcraft because it leads to idolatry. In Deuteronomy 29:27 we read: **And the anger of the LORD was kindled against this land, to bring upon it all the curses that are written in this book.** In Exodus 20:3 God commands: **Thou shalt have no other gods before me.**

The Bible says that the gods of the heathen are devils. The Lord doesn't want devils before Him. They are fallen angels whom He has cast out of heaven, so He doesn't want them in His presence whatsoever.

The pagans would offer their children to gods and burn them in the fire. God expressly forbids such practices. He says that those who do such things are an abomination to Him. That means they cannot go to heaven, because nothing abominable is allowed there. People must rid themselves of their abominations before they can be acceptable to God. Witchcraft is not harmless; it is an abomination to God and condemns those who engage in it.

Entire nations can lose their land because of this sin. God permits other nations to overwhelm them, to carry them away into captivity and bondage because of their witchcraft.

So few people appreciate how God really feels about alien entities. That's because they have never felt God's anger toward these beings. They have taken God's place. They are gods.

In 1 Corinthians 10:20 Paul writes: **But I say, that the things which the Gentiles sacrifice, they sacrifice to devils, and not to God: and I would not that ye should have fellowship with devils.**

Seeking assistance from witchcraft is calling upon another god. It is insulting to God. In Deuteronomy 18:9-12 He states:

> **When thou art come into the land which the LORD thy God giveth thee, thou shalt not learn to do after the abominations of those nations.**
>
> **There shall not be found among you any one that maketh his son or his daughter to pass through the fire, or that useth divination, or an observer of times, or an enchanter, or a witch,**
>
> **Or a charmer, or a consulter with familiar spirits, or a wizard, or a necromancer.**
>
> **For all that do these things are an abomination unto the LORD: and because of these abominations the LORD thy God doth drive them out from before thee.**

Because of spiritual contamination by demon power, God commanded the children of Israel: **Thou shalt not suffer a witch to live** (Ex. 22:18). It is amazing that the same God Who tells us in John 3:16 that He loved the world so much that He gave His only begotten Son to save the world, should here mete out capital punishment to witches, sorcerers and wizards.

Why is that? Why is God so angry at witchcraft? God is angry at witchcraft because it challenges Him in every form. It is Satan's challenge to the Most High God, his attempt to be like God.

In Isaiah 47:13 God answers this challenge: **Thou art wearied in the multitude of thy counsels. Let now the astrologers, the stargazers, the monthly prognosticators, stand up, and save thee from these things that shall come upon thee.**

What a challenge from the heart of God! If you are going to practice witchcraft, if you are going to consult fortune tellers to give you advice about the future, if you are going to look to the stars for your help, God says, "Then let them save you!"

Astrology is not new. It's been around a long time. I've never been able to understand it. How can anyone believe that a piece of stardust could influence his life here on earth?

The Web

The history of empires teaches us today that witchcraft forms a web of occultism around the victim and will never let loose except by God's power.

Witchcraft can be so subtle. You can seek to commune with the spirit world through home games and unexpectedly become a victim of oppression or possession. Sometimes a person's activities in witchcraft happened many years ago and then its course comes to light. This is true of Ouija boards, automatic writing, crystal balls, voodoo, yoga meditation, fetishes, fortune telling and so forth.

The victim slowly begins to understand his bondage by a spirit of gloominess, or unexpected depression, or uncontrollable passions, or tantrums, obsessions out of character with his real person. Then can come resentments, delusions, compulsive lying, threats of self-destruction. Not the devil has a stronghold.

I have met some people who had terrible feelings against the blood of Jesus or against God or against the Bible or the Holy Spirit. Such people do not respond to medical or psychological treatment. They do not respond to regular prayer, because beyond this witchcraft is an alien entity. It is hidden information and knowledge that is wrong and a lie. Man is only attracted to it by its glamour of supernaturalism.

Human Security

In Ephesians 6:11,12 we are told by the Holy Spirit:

> **Put on the whole armour of God, that ye may be able to stand against the wiles of the devil.**
>
> **For we wrestle not against flesh and blood, but against principalities, against powers, against the rulers of the darkness of this world, against spiritual wickedness in high places.**

As Christians our battle is not against other humans, but against the forces of darkness, against spiritual enemies. We cannot depend upon human power or resources if we are to be victorious over these alien entities. Our security must be in the spiritual armor and weapons of the Lord God of hosts.

The Answer to Witchcraft

**Ye are of God, little children, and have overcome
them** (evil spirits): **because greater is he that is in you,
than he that is in the world.**

1 John 4:4

This means that any negative power or entity can
be exorcized from any human. A Christian can defeat,
expel, and cast out any alien entity.

The last words Jesus spoke on the face of this earth
were these: **And these signs shall follow them that
believe; In my name shall they cast out devils...** (Mark
16:17).

This was not spoken to any particular people. It
was not spoken just for ministers or for priests. It was
spoken to lay people also. They that believe have a
right to do it. You have a right to set people free.

You need not refer people to someone else for
help. As a believer you can help them yourself. *You*
can do it. Wherever you are, you are God's minister.
And He wants you to set people free from spiritual
bondage.

11

Is a Nervous Breakdown the Work of an Alien Entity?

And the peace of God, which passeth all understanding, shall keep your hearts and minds through Christ Jesus.

Philippians 4:7

There are some people who blame everything that happens on the devil. They remind me of a little story I heard once about a man who saw the devil sitting on the curb outside a little church, crying.

"What are you crying about, devil?" the man asked.

"Oh, they just blame *everything* on me in there!" the devil bemoaned.

Well, despite all that we have said thus far about Satan and his activities there are some things we don't have to blame on him. Some things in life are a direct result of people's own actions, or lack of action.

A nervous breakdown, for example, is not necessarily a sign of being possessed of the devil, although emotional problems and demonic possession are related and intertwined. When a person has a natural weakness, such as a nervous disorder or even a blow to the head, the devil may take advantage of that situation to move in and try to possess the person. When a person has no strength to resist Satan, he will take advantage of the situation, even though he may not be the primary cause of it to begin with.

Philippians 4:7 speaks of the peace of God which passes all understanding. There are millions of people who need the peace of God in their lives today. Not the peace of a nation, or the peace of a good job, not even the peace of financial security or success, but the peace of God. There is a peace that comes from God.

We learn from Romans 14:17 that, **the kingdom of God is...righteousness, and peace, and joy in the Holy Ghost.** The peace of God is a gift to man. It is part of his redemption, his new birth. It comes into his being when he is born again.

If you have been born again, then you are peace. You don't just have peace, you *are* peace, because your peace is the peace of God. His peace is beyond comprehension. It passes all understanding.

The Bible says that the peace of God can keep you. It can keep your heart and your mind. When troubles and problems come, and everything breaks down, that's the time to stand on the knowledge that God's peace reigns supreme in your life. God gives peace, we are peace, but we must remain in that peace.

We understand that half the hospital beds in our land today are occupied by people with severe emotional disorders. There seems to be a remarkable acceleration of emotional sickness in our generation. Americans have less to be disturbed about than any people on the face of the earth. Yet we are plagued by emotional sickness. Why? What causes emotional disorder?

First, let's consider what a nervous breakdown really is. A nervous breakdown is closely related to a person's soulical parts: mind, emotions, and will.

A nervous breakdown is remarkably related to man's Adamic nature. From this nature he received a potential for his mental power, his emotional power, and the powers of his will. It is possible for all three of these soulical units or factors to become involved in what medical science calls a nervous breakdown.

The mind can go, so that the person cannot think and do his work.

His emotions can go, so he can no longer control them.

And his will can go, so he just sits in a corner, not moving, in an almost catatonic state.

When a person's spirit becomes the king of his life, when he is born again, that spirit is supposed to dominate those soulical parts.

I don't like to say this, but it is true. I don't see how a Christian can have a nervous breakdown, because his born-again spirit is telling his mind to think straight. His spirit is telling his emotions to calm down. That spirit tells his will to speak to God and declare, "Not my will, but Thy will be done." How can anyone have a nervous breakdown in that situation?

Yet I know some beautiful people who have had a nervous breakdown. Why? What went wrong? The answer lies in one of the three soulical areas.

The Mind

The nervous system of the human is closely related to the brain. The great masses of nerves move up from the trunk of the body to the brain. In a nervous break-down, a person's mind is certainly affected. He cannot cope with his responsibilities and he cannot accept challenges to achieve.

The Emotions

A person's emotions are also closely related to the brain. For example, anxiety or depression is affected by the emotional area of the human, but is also related to his brain functions. Emotional abilities can reflect joy and gladness or sorrow and sadness. Emotions can reveal deep-rooted fears or the power of living faith.

There are literally hundreds of human emotions. They must all be in full control of the human mind.

Isaiah, the great prophet, said of God: **Thou wilt keep him in perfect peace, whose mind is stayed on thee: because he trusteth in thee** (Is. 26:3). If your mind is stayed upon God, then you have perfect peace. If it is on disaster or probabilities, you won't have peace. It's just that simple.

I have been building a new sermon on the case of probabilities. If someone were to ask if you were going to church next Sunday, or if you were going to buy a new car in the future, you would most likely say, "Probably." That is normal, that's the way our human mind works. But the Word of God does not deal in probabilities, it deals in absolutes. That's why those who build their lives upon it can continually experience the peace of God.

The Will

The third area of the soulical parts is the human will. It functions in close relationship to the emotions and the mind. The human will of man is powerful, and a man with a strong will holds up longer than the one who gives in easily to pressure.

Inner Strength

Certainly there are many people today who could have what is termed a nervous breakdown if they were to let go of their inner strength and permit their emotions and their mental forces to be loosed from the footings and foundations of a normal person, if they accepted a collapse of their soulical being.

The truth is, when any Christian (especially) has a nervous breakdown, it is because he has permitted it to happen. You may not realize it, but much of our emotional problems come because of self-pity. For one reason or another, people begin to feel sorry for themselves and become depressed and despondent. When they do, they let down their defenses and Satan moves in to take advantage of those negative feelings until he causes an emotional crisis.

Don't ever give in to self-pity, because it is always motivated by Satan. It is one of the devices he uses to try to destroy your emotional stability and rob you of your peace and mental health.

In relation to a nervous breakdown being the work of an alien entity, we must realize that Satan often moves into weakness.

For example, if you are experiencing physical exhaustion, the devil could use that to enter your mind, your emotions and your will. Or if a loved one died, especially if it were a premature death, the devil could prey upon your thought life, your emotional stability and your will power, seeking to destroy you.

The sinner, at this point, has no supernatural assistance. A counselor or a doctor might be of some help. But in order to combat a spiritual enemy, we need spiritual strength and power.

The Bible Answer

In a time of crisis is when the Christian is at his best. The Christian spirit, his "born-again" nature, is his divine connection with the Godhead. It reaches out from its throne in the midst of the human frame and speaks positively to the mind, saying: "Hold steady. Don't be blown about by every wind of doctrine. Don't believe every spirit. Try the spirits."

Then the spirit, the born-again spirit of man, reaches over to the emotions and says: "Don't drop into melancholy and depression. Don't spit anger out of your emotional labyrinth; subdue it—speak love to it."

Finally, the spirit speaks to the will of the human soul and demands stability rather than indecision and double-mindedness. The spirit demands the soul to rest in the faithfulness of the Most High.

Then God's Word begins to speak: **The Lord is my shepherd; I shall not want. He maketh me to lie down in green pastures: he leadeth me beside the still waters. He restoreth my soul....** The 23rd Psalm is the best deterrent I know to a nervous breakdown.

Most nervous breakdowns certainly are not related to demon power. But unless these negative thoughts and emotions are controlled by the power of the Word of God, it is easy to fall prey to Satan's attacks.

God is not pleased with a nervous breakdown. As we have stated, nervous breakdowns are usually built upon self-pity, sometimes upon falsehood, and always upon a lack of trust in the love and power of Almighty God. They are the hiding places for sorrows.

We, as Christians, must resist nervous breakdown just as we resist any other attack of the devil, **for we are not ignorant of his devices** (2 Cor. 2:11).

12

Is Schizophrenia an Alien Entity?

For God hath not given us the spirit of fear; but of power, and of love, and of a sound mind.

2 Timothy 1:7

When Paul speaks of *us* in this verse, he is referring to the Body of Christ, the believers, the redeemed of the Lord. God has not given born-again, Spirit-filled people the spirit of fear.

Notice the words *spirit of fear*. We don't believe the Bible makes mistakes. Fear in its ultimate is a spirit, not in its primary stages. In its primary stages, fear is believing a lie.

Foolish parents tell their children: "There's a boogie-man in that room. If you go in there, the boogie-man will get you." It is wrong to teach such things to innocent little children, to create fear in them, fears they may carry throughout their entire lives.

God is not a God of fear. He is a God of liberty and freedom. He sets people free from fear and gives them joy. Fear has no joy in it, only terror. Therefore, fear is not from God.

A spirit of fear is the ultimate reality of fear. That's when fear has become master, when it dominates a person's life, throwing his soulical parts (mind, emotions, and will power) out of focus. When that happens, the person can no longer see things properly or as they really are.

God has not given us a spirit of fear, but the spirit of power, the spirit of love, and the spirit of a sound mind. Who is it who has a sound mind? Who has the power to think clearly today, tomorrow, and for eternity? The man who is born again knows who he is, where he came from, and where he is going. The sinner does not know that because he does not have that strong spiritual foundation of power and love and a sound mind. That is why he is so susceptible to fear, worry, anxiety and every kind of mental and emotional disorder.

The medical world states that schizophrenic disorders of the human mind are greatly on the increase. It is sad that in our modern world, with all its sophisticated technology, we have an increase of something which should be decreasing. The reason is because these things do not come from without, but from within, from moral and spiritual causes.

It is believed by medical scientists that schizophrenics possess dual or multiple personalities. They identify schizophrenia by action and reaction as compared to normal and accepted behavior. Simply stated, schizophrenia is a mental disorder characterized by a splitting of the human personality, disassociation from positive actions, and/or emotional deterioration.

The Size of the Problem

About 30 million Americans suffer from schizophrenia or other psychiatric problems; 1.5 million Americans require hospitalization due to their mental torments. This is an army of people, human beings we Christians need to help and bless and love.

The Treatment

Medical science, through its public mental health system, deals with this problem in various ways. Its attempts to help include:

1. Electroshock therapy.

2. Insulin therapy.

3. Drug therapy, such as antipsychotic, antidepressant, antimanic and mega-vitamin treatments.

Medical scientists freely admit that there is no positive or sure cure for schizophrenia and other sorts of mental illness.

The Terms

Doctors have almost produced a dictionary of terms to describe human mental problems.

For example, science says that mentally ill people suffer from one or more of these disorders or symptoms:

1. Schizophrenia: From two Greek words meaning "split" and "mind." A mental disorder characterized by a splitting of the personality, disorganized thinking, and an inability to distinguish factual reality.

2. Psychosis: Any major, severe form of mental affection or disease. A **psychotic** suffers from abnormal mind.

3. Paranoia: A mental disorder in which the person affected ascribes his own delusions and personal conflicts to the supposed hostility of others.

Such a person is said to be **paranoid.**

4. Dementia: A mental disorder characterized by impairment or loss of the mental powers. A **demented person** is commonly said to be "out of his mind."

5. Neurosis: A mental illness marked by obsessive thoughts, compulsive acts and physical complaints without objective evidence of disease. The affected person is called a **neurotic,** a term also used to pertain to nerves or nervous disease affecting the mental attitude.

6. Hallucinations: Illusions or false notions caused by an inability of the mind to perceive reality.

7. Maladjustment: A mental condition in which one's personality or thinking is out of balance. Such a person is said to be **maladjusted.**

8. Eccentricity: The quality of being **eccentric,** or deviating from the recognized or usual character, practice, etc.; irregular; erratic; peculiar; odd; etc.

9. Delusions: False mental conceptions resistant to reason.

10. Catatonia: A syndrome of a mental disorder most frequently seen in schizophrenia, with muscular rigidity, and mental stupor, sometimes alternating with great excitement and confusion. A person in this condition is said to be **catatonic.**

11. Hebephrenia: A form of dementia praecox incidental to the age of puberty, characterized by childish behavior, hallucinations, and emotional deterioration.

12. Mania: A form of insanity characterized by great excitement, with or without delusions, and in its acute stage by great violence. The **maniac** is described as being wildly insane, raving mad, a madman.

13. Amnesia: Loss of memory. The person affected is **amnesic** or **amnestic.**

14. Pseudoneurosis: A mental disorder involving serious thought disturbances and found to be severely disabling.

15. Hysteria: A mental disorder characterized by violent emotional outbursts, perversion of sensory and motor functions, and various morbid effects due to auto-suggestion.

16. Depersonalization: The loss of one's personal expression or characteristic personality.

17. Derealization: The loss of the ability to distinguish the real world from the imaginary.

18. Disassociation: A split in the conscious process, as if belonging to another person.

These are some of the terms you would find in any book on schizophrenia. They are terms you will have to come to understand if you deal with this subject in any depth. Ministers should study these at length, as well as other related areas of mental and emotional disorder, because they will have to deal with them extensively in ministering to people in need.

The Soulical Problem

Schizophrenia is a soulical problem affecting the mind, emotions and will. This means that it is not of the spirit of man; his body is only the victim.

The soulical human is made up of the:

1. Mind

2. Emotions

3. Will

Schizophrenia attacks all three of these areas.

The Effects

The problem begins mostly in the mind. The devil hates the mind because it is the throne of the human personality. He strives to take over that throne. As he does, the human mind refuses certain forms of reality. This mental instability then affects the emotions. The attendant fears, angers, outrages, and tears become outbursts of unreality.

Then the disorder begins to affect the will to do and to be.

Loved ones and friends are baffled. They seek medical assistance for the victim, but often this terminates in a broken home or family situation.

When the schizophrenic is sent away to a hospital for the mentally deranged, other members of the family are burdened with feelings of guilt, sadness, and the eternal question of why it happened.

Is Schizophrenia an Alien Entity?

It is probable that a person with a dual personality is tormented by an alien entity. Schizophrenia is certainly an abnormal mental torment.

Often we know what a thing is by what it does. For example, does a schizophrenic love God and show it? Is he or she as sociable as other members of the family? Does the schizophrenic rise to high levels of achievement? Is he or she a leader in the community?

The answer to these questions would help identify schizophrenia. I've never personally known a person with a split personality to be a real spiritual leader. Schizophrenia has no apparent benefits for the affected person. This reveals to us that schizophrenia is not of God.

Except for children who are born abnormal, I do not believe that Satan can get a firm hold upon a person, to the extent of schizophrenia, unless he is permitted to do so. The Bible tells us to resist the devil and he will flee from us: **Submit yourselves therefore to God. Resist the devil, and he will flee from you** (James 4:7).

This means that from our youth we should try to be like Jesus in all our actions, and to resist the devil in all areas of our life. In so doing, we discover the secret to a normal mental life.

Some schizophrenics are born mentally maladjusted. Sometimes, especially in the heathen world, certain people are born possessed of the devil. Arlindo Oliveira, the witch doctor from Brazil, for example, was baptized and dedicated to the devil in a voodoo worship ceremony before he was born. So there are strange abnormalities, physical and mental, which can come at birth.

But most often a broken personality is the result of decisions which were made by the person involved. However, I would not say that a person considered to have a split personality must necessarily be demon possessed. It might be that he is only oppressed of the devil, in accordance with Acts 10:38: ...**Jesus of Nazareth...went about doing good, and healing all that were oppressed of the devil....**

Deliverance from Mental Illness

In a case of healing a person of schizophrenia, the minister or the one who prays would need to possess divine authority to rebuke the oppression and set the sick person free.

I know from many experiences that Christ can heal a mental illness as simply as He can heal a physical illness. Because He designed and created the entire human personality, no human need is beyond His healing and helping hand.

The healing of the Gadarene demoniac in Mark 5:2-15 and the epileptic boy in Luke 9:38-42 are two outstanding examples. Christ cast the alien entities out of them and sent them back to their homes and families. Whatever Jesus could do and did do, the Church can do and does do. So we can deliver people from mental illness, whether it is simple oppression by a demon power or whether it is a case of total demon possession.

Deal with it as it is. Humbly. Spiritually. Positively. Let God set people free through you. After all, He is in the freedom business.

According to Acts 10:38, Jesus went about doing good and healing *all* that were oppressed (and possessed) of the devil, **for God was with him.**

God is with you too, as a believer. That is your assurance of success.

13
Are Witch Doctors Possessed of Alien Entities?

There shall not be found among you any one that maketh his son or his daughter to pass through the fire, or that useth divination, or an observer of times, or an enchanter, or a witch.

Deuteronomy 18:10

In our study, we have seen that alien entities are fallen angels which fell from heaven when Lucifer was cast out. They are now the ones causing hurt to humanity. Although their attacks on the human race cause harm and injury, in reality alien entities have no particular interest in us humans. We are neutral as far as they are concerned. They neither like nor dislike us, of ourselves. We don't mean a thing to them personally.

Nor to Satan. He has no feelings one way or the other about human beings because he has never been a human. He has no idea how you and I feel about anything. He only knows that he was thrown out of heaven, that he will ultimately be cast into hell, and that he hates God.

But because he hates God so much, and because he knows that God loves us humans, he has set out to hurt us to get back at God. Since Satan cannot harm God, his only alternative is to hurt His children. When

Satan comes against you and me, he is actually coming against God. You and I are in the center of a cosmic warfare.

Because the devil unleashes his fury at God on humans, God Himself became one of us to save us from His enemy. The reason Jesus Christ had to become a man was because, otherwise, He would never have known us personally. If He had remained God, He would never have known what it was like to be human. He could not have known us until he was clothed in flesh so that His body could feel pain as ours do. When Jesus became tired, then He could identify with us and understand our fatigue. When His stomach ached with emptiness, He learned what it was to be hungry. When He became a man, Jesus learned how human beings feel and what they experience.

It was necessary for Jesus to experience humanity so He could become our High Priest in heaven, **For we have not an high priest which cannot be touched with the feeling of our infirmities...** (Heb. 4:15).

Jesus had to be denied by Peter so He could know what denial was. He had to go through the Judas experience of betrayal, so He could know what we feel as humans when we are betrayed by our friends. Everything that Jesus suffered as a man, He suffered because we suffer, and to overcome the one who causes that suffering so that we might live victoriously over him through Jesus' Name and the power of His blood.

Therefore, the whole message of alien entities is that they are out to hurt God through you and me because we are the apple of God's eye. Once we have these things in their proper perspective, we understand better how to live, how to defeat Satan in his attacks, how to live victoriously over him.

Witch Doctor Possessed of Alien Entities

A question which always arises in any study of alien entities concerns witch doctors: Are witch doctors possessed of alien entities? In order to answer that question, let's look again at one of these witch doctors, Arlindo Barbosa de Oliveira of Brazil.

Arlindo's story was so amazing I invited him to America and had him tell it in Carnegie Hall, New York City, in Constitution Hall, Washington, D.C., and in auditoriums from Florida to the state of Washington. This type of revelation ministry was a little before its time. If I could do it again today, there would be thousands of people in attendance at these meetings. In that case, there were only a few hundred who came to hear him because at that point in time, America was not yet awakened to the reality and the danger of alien activity. This man knew all about the subject.

At the time I met Arlindo, he worked in the office of the President of Brazil, and had worked in the Ministry of War and other government agencies of that nation. I point out this fact to show that a person can be possessed of the devil and still hold a good job. Arlindo, for example, fulfilled a high government position by day and was a witch doctor by night—for 40 years!

We must remember that we are not talking about insane people when we talk of witchcraft. Many of the people involved in this demonic activity are well-educated, intelligent, successful human beings, which makes them all the more dangerous and all the more difficult to identify.

Over a period of years I have come to know Arlindo well. He knows more about witchcraft than any person I have ever met. His deliverance from witchcraft by a persistent Protestant pastor is an amazing story in itself.

One day when Arlindo came home from work, he found that his wife had packed up and left him. She just couldn't stand the devil in him anymore, so she moved out. She took all the furniture, the stove, the bed, everything she could. The house was almost bare. Arlindo never found her.

Since he had no other place to stay, Arlindo moved in with his sister, who happened to be a member of a Full Gospel church. The pastor of that church lived right next door. As soon as he learned that Arlindo was a witch doctor, the pastor set in to free him from his demon possession. He persistently rebuked the devil in him until he set him free.

Thank God for men of courage who will do that. Now this man was not a celebrated minister, just the humble pastor of a church with fewer than 200 members. But he set a powerful witch doctor free. That's what we want to see more and more in this country.

In my seminars, people will sometimes travel seven or eight hundred miles to be prayed over. No one should ever have to go more than five blocks to find deliverance. Some servant of the Most High ought to be right there in the neighborhood to set them free.

Dedicated to the Devil at Birth

As mentioned previously in this book, Arlindo was dedicated to the devil before he was born. His mother, a Macumba spiritist, dedicated him to a special and strong demon prince before his birth. A few days before Arlindo's birth, a reputable witch doctor put hot chicken blood (the chicken's head was cut off before the ceremony) on his mother's stomach. The blood was placed in the form of a cross. (Spiritists often use religious symbols, even Christian symbols, in their rituals; but with perverted meanings.) Arlindo's mother then heard a masculine voice from her belly saying, "He is my son."

By the time Arlindo was three years old, alien entities were moving within him very strongly. He was unruly and disobedient. A spirit manifested in him called Dr. Reubenstein. The spirit said it had manifested in a German doctor in a former life. When this spirit manifested, Arlindo, at three years of age, would write prescriptions in Latin. Sick people took these prescriptions to the druggist and he could read them. This caused Arlindo to be both hated and praised.

300 Devils Within

I once asked Arlindo how many spirits had manifested in him in his lifetime and he replied that there were at least 300 that he knew by name. I asked him which spirits manifested in him most often. These are the ones he mentioned.

1. Oxala (oh-chal-ah)—The head of all spirits.

2. Oxun (oh-chun)—A female spirit identified with the Virgin Mary.

3. Obum (oh-boom)—Known as St. George.

4. Oxafun (oh-chal-ah-foon)—Also called The Holy Spirit.

5. Oxaci (oh-schassi)—Prayed to as St. Sebastian.

6. Abaliuet or St. Lazarus—King of the cemeteries. Arlindo said that when Abaliuet manifested himself, he would twist Arlindo's body so terribly that his assistants would have to pour oil on his limbs and work with them to straighten out the contorted joints. Abaliuet made him eat meat which had been left in the sun until it was rotten. Arlindo had to wash it down with olive oil.

7. Quinca Araviei Sara—This spirit was crippled and limped. He had a wife.

Some devils manifested themselves rarely, perhaps only once a year. Others called themselves by such titles as "King of the Sun," "King of Man," "The Morning Star," etc.

From Arlindo we learn that the world is divided into zones. Various spirits rule over different zones, such as the jungle, forests, seas, rivers, and other areas set off by natural boundaries.

I asked Arlindo who was the king of all the alien entities he knew. Arlindo said that all the witchcraft sects in Brazil consider Oxala (oh-chal-ah) the head of all spirits.

Arlindo, a handsome black man, said with a strong voice: "The devils spoiled my life. I never had a normal childhood because of the devils in me, and I never knew the love of a mother or a father.

"When I went to school, the spirits would make trouble. They wouldn't let me study and they caused me to fight with the teacher. When the teacher would give me work to do, a spirit would give the answer before the teacher was through presenting the problem. This would make her angry. Then the spirit would speak through my lips saying I knew more than she. This would make her even more angry.

"One day when I was just eight years old, a spirit manifested in me while in school, and I began to argue with the teacher. The spirit said, ''You are the teacher, but I know more than you do.' The teacher complained to the principal, and I was discharged from school."

By the time Arlindo was sixteen years old the alien entities were very strong in him. He would often faint on the street. Once he was picked up and taken by ambulance to the hospital and then to jail. At this time Arlindo was back living with his parents. One night a spirit manifested in him and he did not come home until 2:00 a.m.

Arlindo says, "My father met me and said, 'What kind of an hour of the night is this to come home?' "

Arlindo remembers that the spirit replied to his father, "It's no business of yours."

"This angered my father," says Arlindo, "and he spoke bitterly to me. But the arrogant entity in me argued back. My father reached for a piece of wood to strike me. The demon entity said, 'If you are a man, you can hit me with that.'

"But my father's arm became frozen in mid-air and he could not bring it down. 'What are you?' my father asked.

"The spirit from within me responded, 'I am Summa Quis Summa Qua (Sooma). I lived long before you.'

"My father did not believe until the spirit told how he was the spirit who gave the enchantment which made it possible for my father to get my mother to marry him when she did not want to do so. My father broke down and confessed that the spirit was right and that he now believed in the spirit. After that my father supported me and my spirit work."

According to Arlindo, the entity Summa Quis Summa Qua also said that he originally was an African who had died at the age of 165. This spirit claimed that he had previously lived in 350 persons.

The entities which dealt with Arlindo were mostly the chiefs of legions. One of these, named "Skullbones" or "Crossbones," called Arlindo "my apparatus." In other words, what this spirit was saying to Arlindo was, "I operate through you. I control your body to accomplish my own desires."

Anyone who permits the devil to function through him becomes his apparatus, his tool, his slave!

A person can serve the devil all his life, but Satan has no affection for that person at all. To Satan he is nothing more than a machine to be used until it wears out and is discarded. Satan has no feeling of loyalty toward those who serve him. People in countries such as India have served him for centuries, yet one generation means no more to him than the last.

"Crossbones" made Arlindo eat roaches, which he called "shrimp." He made him eat poisonous toads.

Arlindo says this spirit made him cut himself with a dagger, and then pour rum over the wounds. He was in terrible condition when Jesus found him through the Protestant minister.

This same spirit cursed Arlindo's mother because he said that she drank his rum. Arlindo reports that this spirit had an unhealing sore on his foot.

Why is Spiritism Evil?

Arlindo says that spiritism keeps people poor. Condomble, a strong form of witchcraft, uses mostly blood sacrifices, usually obtained from chickens, sheep, goats and other animals, but also from humans.

Spiritism demands costly clothes and costumes. The spirit, Eixu, made Arlindo buy an expensive outfit just to please him. Some devils demand a golden sword or they will not manifest themselves.

Spiritism teaches people not to believe in Judgment Day or the end of the world. Instead, it teaches reincarnation. All spirits live forever, they say, they are born again and again. Spirits never speak of sin, just of "faults." Neither do they speak of faith, they know nothing of it. The leading spirits told Arlindo that they had never died and that they were created and had lived before Jesus.

One time Arlindo was invited to a great witchcraft dancing session where some 4,000 witchcraft followers and hundreds of witch doctors were present. He did not find the dances very good; most of the dancers did not manifest demon power but were just doing it themselves. Finally, because he found fault with the dancing, Arlindo was asked to show what he could do. He danced for hours by the power of spirits.

As a result, an American dancer who was there to study witchcraft dances chose Arlindo to teach her. For several months he taught the American to dance the Macumba dances. He trained her also to have the spirits manifest in her to help her to dance. He danced as her partner in a number of nightclubs in Rio de Janeiro.

Some popular American dancers have gone to the devil to learn demon dances. They show them on the American stage, films and television. Many people learn these dances and practice them with no idea of their origin and real meaning and purpose.

When asked if the spirits ever showed kindness or affection, even to their mediums, Arlindo said, "There has never been an alien entity who had any affection for any human being." He went on to say that they would help a person and even protect him for a while, but they showed no personal interest in him at all. They never showed any kindness or love for any human.

Therefore, from what we have learned from such people as Arlindo de Oliveira, we must conclude that witch doctors are indeed possessed of alien entities. As Christians we must heed God's warning in His Word and avoid all contact with the forces of darkness.

14

Can Alien Entities Manifest Themselves Physically?

Be sober, be vigilant; because your adversary the devil, as a roaring lion, walketh about, seeking whom he may devour.

1 Peter 5:8

In teaching, it is always good to have a truth to expound. It is also good to have illustrations of that truth so it will be fully understood.

Many times the only thing religious teachers can present is doctrine with no experiential evidence to back it up. Without such evidence, there is no proof of the doctrine. It remains only speculation, only theory, something which may sound good but which cannot be proven.

The purpose of this specific lesson is not only to present a doctrine or a truth, but also to present factual evidence of what took place when that truth was applied to a real-life situation.

The Strange Story of Clarita Villanueva

Clarita Villanueva, a 17-year-old Filipina girl, had known a life of tragedy. She did not remember her father. She did not know if he had died or had deserted her mother.

Her mother was a spiritist and a fortune teller by vocation. The girl was brought up watching her mother holding seances, communicating with the dead, and using clairvoyance to predict to sinful people what they could expect in the future. Her mother took money from people for her services, and then laughed at them behind their backs. To her it was all just a game, a means of making a living by duping unsuspecting and gullible people.

When Clarita was still very young, about twelve years old, her mother died. Since she did not have any immediate family to take her in and care for her, she became a vagabond. She fell into the hands of harlots and at the tender age of 12 was selling her body as a prostitute. The harlots taught her how to handle men, how to get money for her services.

Clarita worked her way up from her island home to the capital city of Manila. The big city was a hiding place, a center of money and vice for her business. The local harlots became her teachers and she learned the night life in the big capital city. In Manila there were more men to seduce. By the time she was 17 years old, Clarita was frequenting the bars and taverns of Manila, living the ''gay life'' by soliciting men for harlotry.

But one morning at 2 a.m. on the streets of downtown Manila, Clarita made the mistake of offering her services to a plainclothes police officer. The policeman called for a vehicle and Clarita was taken to the ancient Bilibid Prison, used as the city jail. Bilibid has been a prison for over 300 years. It was built by the Spanish and used by the Americans, the Filipinos, and the Japanese as a prison and a place of torment.

Two days after Clarita was incarcerated, there struck the strangest phenomenon to ever hit Bilibid Prison in its 300-year history. This young harlot was bitten severely on her body by unseen and unknown alien entities. There were two of them—a huge monster-like spirit and a smaller one. They sunk their fangs and teeth deep into her flesh making deep indentations. They would bite her neck, back, legs and arms simultaneously. Blood flowed, mostly underneath her skin, from the bites. The 17-year-old girl screamed in horror and fainted.

The guards and medics heard the commotion and came running to the women's division of the prison. The other female inmates pointed to the writhing, tormented girl on a cot.

The girl was taken to the prison hospital for observation and treatment where all the doctors declared that they had never seen anything like it.

These strange demonic bitings began to occur daily, baffling all who saw it. Dr. Lara, the prison physician, appealed for help through the media and permitted many to view the strange phenomenon. Filipino, Chinese and American doctors, university professors, and other professionals were called in to analyze the situation.

The news media soon caught wind of the occurrence and sent reporters out to investigate. The newspapers, radio stations and magazines found it their kind of story and began to publicize it. Even the cartoonists were soon drawing pictures of the entities from Clarita's descriptions, as the bitings continued day by day. The UPI and other world news services began to report the phenomenon worldwide.

In my travels throughout the world, I have not been in any country in which the newspapers did not give this story front-page coverage. Switzerland, France, Germany, England, Canada, the United States—everywhere this strange phenomenon was front-page news at the time.

One doctor accused the girl of putting on an act in order only to get publicity. Clarita gazed at the doctor. With her snake-like eyes she said, "You will die." He didn't feel anything at the moment, but the following day the doctor expired without even getting sick. He simply died. Fear struck the city when that news was spread about. The girl was not only a harlot, they said, she was also a witch who could speak curses upon human beings and they would die.

The chief jailer had a confrontation with the girl. He had kicked her for something she had done wrong while rebelling against him. Clarita looked at the jailer in cold, inhuman hate and said, "You will die!" Within four days the man was dead and buried, the second person to fall victim to her curse.

I walked into Bilibid Prison just as the funeral cortege moved out. The prison guards had paid their last respects to their chief. Dr. Lara, the chief medical officer, and his staff were deeply concerned. They had a prisoner who certainly was not crazy, but who was being wildly attacked by unseen entities and being bitten deeply on all parts of her body by creatures no one else could see. I have never seen such a fearful and perplexed group of people as those I met in that prison that day. They were afraid that this thing would kill them as it had the two others who dared cross it. It was their responsibility to do something for the girl, yet they had no earthly idea what to do about the situation. It was beyond their medical knowledge.

Who were these alien entities? The large one, Clarita said, was a monster in size. He was black and very hairy. He had fangs that came down on each side of his mouth, plus a set of buck-teeth all the way around. The doctors verified her description by the teeth marks on her body: buck-teeth solid, all the way around the bite, rather than sharp teeth in the front.

The smaller entity was almost like a dwarf. He would climb up her body to bite her upper torso. Both of these spirits liked to bite her where there was a lot of flesh, like the back of her leg, the back of her neck, the fleshy part of her upper arms. They would bite deep into her, leaving ugly, painful bruises.

Dr. Lara and his medical assistants called in all sorts of observers, medical doctors, surgeons, psychiatrists and professors from the Far East University and the University of Santo Tomas. No one had ever witnessed such strange and demonic behavior. Nor did they know any solution to the problem. They all wondered who would be the next victim of her curse.

Dr. Lara and his staff sent out word everywhere, "Come and help us. Please help us." They received 3,000 cables from heathen countries suggesting possible cures, but not one from a Christian country.

Do you see how we Christians have been asleep? The word went out over the world. Three thousand telegrams came in, mostly from Japan and India, telling them what to do with an invisible biting monster. But not one Christian nation had any solution to the problem.

They asked in Manila for somebody to come and help. The only group who turned up were the spiritists who said it was John the Baptist biting her. The officials asked the spiritists to leave.

I was the next one to come upon the scene. After three awful weeks of this torture, a radio reporter came to Bilibid and taped a session while the doctors were violently struggling with the demonized harlot. The reporter immediately released his story on a local radio station, just after the 10 o'clock news.

This was the first I had heard of the hell in Bilibid Prison. The newspapers had given it front-page coverage, but I was too busy building a church to read the newspapers. That's what the devil would like for us to do, to get so involved in taking care of our own little mission that we allow him a free rein to do anything he wants to do.

When the Bible says to be vigilant, this is what it means: to see what the devil is doing in the world; to keep up with him; to resist him and fight him in whatever he might be doing.

I stayed up all night praying and weeping before the Lord. I was interceding for the city, for the girl and for myself. I was living in a city that had a great need and I was not helping to meet that need. I was so busy putting up our church building and doing my own thing that I was not involved in the tragedy of Bilibid. The next morning God spoke to me and told me to go to that prison and pray for the demonized girl. I did not want to go, but God assured me that He had no one else in the city to send. Therefore I went.

Because I was a foreigner in the Philippines, I went to the mayor's office and asked permission to see

Clarita. He granted me his permission but warned me that several people had been injured by the girl and that two had been cursed and were dead. I went with the understanding that I would not sue the government if I was hurt, and that I would not complain if mistreated.

When I arrived at the prison, the head doctor of six physicians, Dr. Lara, was skeptical of this foreign minister, but he finally permitted me to see the girl.

Clarita was brought into a special room where I was waiting with a large group of news reporters, foreign members of the press, university professors, and medical doctors, who had been invited by Dr. Lara.

As Clarita was being led into the room, she looked at them and said nothing, but when she saw me she screamed violently, "I hate you!" Instantly I inserted, "I know you hate me. I have come to cast you out."

That was the beginning of the confrontation. There was a raging battle with the girl blaspheming God the Father, God the Son, and God the Holy Spirit. Her eyes were burning coals of fire and full of hate. I commanded the evil spirit to loose her. After a three-day confrontation with the devil in her, the miracle of God came upon her. She relaxed, smiled, and said, "He's gone."

"Where did he go?" I asked.

"He went out that way," she replied. "He's gone."

The local newspapers, magazines and radio told the story. One headline read, "He dies; the devil is dead!" Another one said, "Devil loses round one."

Dr. Lara became so excited he took me over to the office of the mayor. When he walked into the office, he said, "My God, mayor. The devil is dead."

I said, "Mr. Mayor, Dr. Lara may be a good doctor, but he's a poor theologian. The devil is not dead. The girl I came and talked to you about yesterday is healed."

That did it. Mayor Lacson was delighted. He asked if there was anything he could do for me. He was so grateful and appreciative, he said I could have anything I wanted, just name it.

I said, "There are things that I need all right. I have mechanical drawings in this office for our new church building. To tell you the truth, I have been building some of it without permission because I didn't have enough money to get through your organization here."

The mayor rang a bell. In about 10 minutes he had my plans for a large building. He sat there and stamped and signed them. As he handed them to me, he said, "You're the first Protestant that ever did get anything free in this city. Is there anything else you want?"

I said, "Yes, there is."

"What is it?"

I said, "I would like to preach in Rojas Park, called the Sunken Gardens, across the street."

"For how long?" he asked.

"Oh, about six weeks."

"Six weeks," he replied. "That's a long time."

"Well, it will take a long time to say all I've got to say."

"The girl is healed," he said abruptly. "You can have the park as long as you want it."

So we began to prepare for our great revival meeting. The way God arranged it was just magnificent.

Without even knowing what we were doing, Gordon Lindsay in Texas sent us thousands of magazines with testimonies in them. Also without knowing what we were doing, Oral Roberts sent me a film on healing, complete with a projector, a screen and everything to go with it.

Through Ruben Candelaria, superintendent of the Methodist church in the Manila area, God miraculously opened up the churches of the city to us for sevices. I went to all the main churches preaching, showing the film, and distributing the magazines. By the time we went into the park meetings, the whole city was aflame.

The Taytay Methodist church paid for me to go on the radio. They paid for 15 minutes after the evening news on a powerful station which covered the whole nation. Every night, right after the news, I talked about what was happening in Manila. People came from all over the country to attend the meetings. Not one city was unrepresented. They came to see the miracles that were taking place. Every kind of miracle imaginable was witnessed. For 15 minutes every night I just told how many miracles there had been that day, what God was doing for others, and invited people to come and see for themselves.

The Reverend Clifton Erickson was the evangelist, and we saw the crowds grow from 40 to 50 to 60 thousand people. Among those people, God saved 150,000 human beings! We witnessed the greatest revival that nation has ever known. **The revival remains there until this day, all over that land.**

The remarkable thing is, it all came about through the deliverance of a little nobody, a young harlot in prison. All of these beautiful people, some of them in the highest ranks of society, had their hearts and lives changed because a young girl was delivered.

That gives us the purpose of setting people free. We set them free, not only for their sake, but to move nations for God.

When we talk about these alien entities, it is for a purpose. When God sets somebody free, there is a purpose behind it. The purpose is immortal souls—that we might lead people to God, that we might lead people to heaven.

15

Cornelio Closa, the Disappearing Boy!

And they were all amazed, and spake among themselves, saying, What a word is this! for with authority and power he commandeth the unclean spirits, and they come out.

Luke 4:36

The story of the invisible boy is true. It is a story to which I was intimately related. It is about a young Filipino boy who was tormented by an alien entity for more than a year.

This spirit would cause him to disappear from a classroom at school or from his home. Cornelio's father would nail the doors and windows shut, but Cornelio did not need natural openings to get in and out of the house.

Because of his disappearing from the classroom, the boy's school teacher had a nervous breakdown and never recuperated sufficiently to teach again. I have personally talked to her and Cornelio's parents. I also visited Cornelio's home. I hired people to check out the validity of this story, including policemen who took signed affidavits about it. We investigated the whole matter very carefully. We didn't want the slightest possibility of falsehood or misrepresentation in it, because we made a film of it. It is surely one of the most well-documented cases in our files.

141

It is interesting to note that a religious leader, Rev. H. A. Baker, traveled from the United States to the Philippines to verify the facts of this case. They were unbelievable to him. But after talking to all of those involved and establishing the facts, he wrote me and said, "Unbeknown to you, I visited the Philippines. I contacted Cornelio, the school teacher, the parents and their neighbors. I discovered that it is absolutely true what you describe about this miracle."

He went on to state: "No doubt, this is the greatest miracle outside of the Bible, and as great as any miracle in the Bible."

Mr. Closa, Cornelio's father and a retired U. S. Navy man, told me, "The first time I noticed something wrong with Cornelio he stayed out late from school. When he came home, he looked troubled and silent.

"When I asked for an explanation of where he had been and who was with him, he would not answer. When I insisted, he growled at me. I took hold of him, but he struggled against my hold and I had to let him go. Then I realized that my son was not himself. He was fighting me for the first time.

"It hurt me because Cornelio had not been a particularly affectionate child. He not only resisted me, but I remember he snarled at me like an animal. I was at a complete loss. I did not know what was happening to Cornelio."

This all happened when Cornelio was about 13 years old. Cornelio's mother remembers: "With every passing day Cornelio became less manageable. I tried everything. I was kind to him. I tried being harsh with him. All I knew was that I had lost control of him. I thought probably it was the bad company he was keeping, so I decided to practically imprison him at home. Cornelio refused to study his lessons. He would sit in one corner of his room, alone, brooding. He would just sit there staring at his plate, refusing to eat.

"One evening Cornelio looked particularly flushed and sick. With the doors and windows locked in the house, Cornelio vanished into thin air, right before my eyes! I was horrified!"

How It Started

Cornelio and a friend were walking home one afternoon cutting across a large open space. Suddenly Cornelio stopped. His eyes were bulging out of their sockets. He was pointing ahead. He said, "See the girl in a long white dress? She is beautiful. She is calling me." Cornelio left his friend and walked forward. Suddenly his friend saw Cornelio disappear from sight. The frightened boy ran home.

"Cornelio began to cause disturbances in school," his teacher told me. "The strange thing about these fights was that Cornelio, as small as he was, would take on three or four boys larger than himself and together the larger boys could not hold him down. He had superhuman strength.

"A few days later, I called him to the front of the class to give the lesson. He went to the blackboard, stood there for a few moments, and then simply evaporated."

His teacher continued, "I was terribly affected by these happenings in my class. I decided before I lost my mind completely, I should resign. I remember how the chain of events made Cornelio laugh and laugh. It was a hideous kind of laugh. It didn't belong to a boy. In fact, it didn't belong to a human being.''

Cornelio said, ''Sleep for me was almost impossible. I was never left to myself. I would perspire profusely. It seemed as if my clothes were burning. Then if I would open my eyes, there would be the face of my friend, looking at me, beckoning me to follow her. Every time her hands touched me I would feel as if I were floating on air. Then I would be gone from home for days. I could not explain to my family just what was wrong. The girl made me promise I would not tell. I just felt tremendous heat in my body.

''Whenever anyone, and that included my parents, spoke to me I would answer rudely or shout. I did not want to snarl, but I could not help myself. If my father punished me, I would fight back. I knew I was displeasing him, but I did not seem to care.

''When no one bothered with me in the house, I would just sit and wait. I did not know why, but I was just waiting for the girl. Many times we would go to the movies and I knew no one could see us.

''Some other times we would eat at restaurants, and when the time came to have to pay, we would conveniently disappear.

''When I was sure no one could see me, I would hide my father's glasses. Without his glasses, my father could not see his hand in front of his eyes. When my parents looked hard enough, they would find their things in the oddest places. When father found his glasses on the transom, he also found his slippers which I had hidden more than a week before.

"With all the traveling that I was doing, I suppose we became very hungry. In the morning the family would find the refrigerator absolutely empty. This was not helping my father's blood pressure. They were sure their invisible boy had been there because the table had been set for two.

"Once my parents forgave me, but then I began stealing money from them. I began taking money from neighbors, even strangers. If I was caught, I fought back.

"I was becoming sickly and pale. I was hungry but I could no longer eat. I would put food in my mouth and I would spit it out. I began breaking dishes and glasses. I wanted to break and smash anything I touched. I knew father was at his wit's end. He tried talking to me once more, but I refused to answer. I pretended to be feeling ill. Then I leaped suddenly in a wild, uncontrolled manner. Father thought I was insane, so he took me to the mental hospital for a check-up.

"We baffled the people at the hospital. The doctors were kind; but while they talked to me about being a good boy, I don't think I was listening.

"Next, father brought me to the correctional institution for juvenile delinquents. Here, I immediately caused trouble. I fought everyone, even the officials. Because of my violent temper, I was often roped to my bed.

"Finally I was returned to my home. My parents seemed to have resigned themselves to living with a monster."

This went on for one entire year, with the situation becoming worse and worse. The parents told me that the whole family would be in the front room of their home and their children would be down on the floor playing. Suddenly, with everybody looking, Cornelio would just disappear. The other children would start coughing and vomiting because of the stench that he would leave behind. When he disappeared, he might be gone for two days or more. Then he might just appear again in bed asleep. He would come in the house without using windows or doors. He would just suddenly be there.

A Ray of Hope

"A ray of hope dawned," says Cornelio, "when a Methodist pastor came to see my father on business and stayed for lunch. It gave my father a chance to ask him how I could be helped with my problem. The pastor took a long look at me, and I scowled at him. I was sure my father was very displeased at the way I was behaving in front of his friend.

"I could hear evil laughter outside the house. It was the alien entity. It was the voice of the girl saying I should run away. The pastor told my father he knew someone who would help me, someone who had helped others. He said I needed help badly and that I had to be prayed for immediately. He told me the devil himself was in my body.

"My parents brought me to church to see Lester Sumrall. The pastor met us there. I was very uncomfortable and wanted to run away.

"The girl made her appearance just outside the church door. She looked different, not pretty anymore, she looked ugly. When she motioned to me, I hid my face. I looked again and she had transformed into something positively horrible and she did not look like a girl, or a woman.

"Reverend Sumrall spoke to the Methodist minister and asked, 'Pastor, what's wrong with this boy?'

"The pastor said, 'He runs away and disappears."

" 'Well, when I was a boy, I used to run away too, but I got a spanking for it.'

" 'He's different,' the pastor responded. 'He may disappear right out of my hands.'

" 'Then it's the devil's power,' Reverend Sumrall said. 'I will pray for him.'

" 'Lord Jesus, we plead Thy holy blood. We command the devil to come out of him. We break the devil's power that this devil can get him no more. May he be surrounded with the blood of Jesus Christ. Be free in Jesus Christ's Name. I believe it. Amen.'

"Then Reverend Sumrall said to me, 'Look up here. Smile. May Christ's blood surround you. The spirit cannot make you disappear again as long as you live.'

"I felt cleansed, purified, and my body was mine again. I joined my parents. And as the song in church rose in glory, I took my place with the people.

"Reverend Sumrall reminded me that there was truly much to be thankful for. I had been in the house of the devil and enslaved to him. Through his help,

Jesus Christ and all His power had made me whole and good again. By the blood of Jesus Christ, by His power without measure and without end, He had saved me from eternal damnation.''

Conclusion

This was Cornelio's witness and testimony. But this is not the end of the story. I always follow up situations like this. I never leave such people on their own after their deliverance. If you do that, you will lose the battle for sure.

The next day I took a pastor with me and we went to the boy's home. We looked at Cornelio. He had not disappeared again. He never did disappear again. We prayed over him once more.

Even though he was just a youngster of 13 or 14, I began to teach him about God. I read to him in the Bible where people were delivered from demon power by the power of God. I told him the thing that had possessed him was nothing but a demon.

He said, ''I believe it now because I saw her face. Otherwise I thought she was an angel. But when I saw her face the last time, it was so demonic, so angry, so hateful. I was so afraid I even put my hands up in front of my face that I might not see her again.''

I talked to the parents. I got them down on their knees. They came through to a beautiful and wonderful salvation. After that they never left our church but worshipped with us all the time.

The boy grew up to be a man in that Christian home. The thing never did torment him again. Of course, we never put this story in the newspapers, but it would have made a tremendous impact because it was one of the greatest miracles of our generation. If the news media had gotten hold of it, it would have been remarkable because of the validity of it. There was so much verification of it that it was impossible for it to have been just a story someone had made up.

I visited Cornelio several years later after he was married. By then he had little children of his own. It was a real pleasure to see that he had stayed well. In fact, he was working for a film company as a cameraman, the same company that made our film about his story. He was happy and very well adjusted in life. God had really made him free.

I would like for you to know that God is able to do the same in our country, in your city and mine. Christ is the same today. He can break and destroy the devil's power and set you free of any satanic hurt that has come into your life. I urge you to let Jesus Christ do it.

He can also use you to set others free. There are yet thousands, perhaps millions, who need deliverance. The Church of Jesus Christ has been commissioned and empowered to bring that deliverance. In John 14:12 Jesus said:

> **Verily, verily, I say unto you, He that believeth on me, the works that I do shall he do also; and greater works than these shall he do; because I go unto my Father.**

The Lord is calling upon us as His ministers to set people free.

16

How I Discovered Alien Entities in Humans

And when he had called unto him his twelve disciples, he gave them power against unclean spirits, to cast them out, and to heal all manner of sickness and all manner of disease.

Matthew 10:1

This chapter delves into the secret passages of my heart. It tells how I became involved in a ministry in which I was not particularly interested at all. If anything, I was averse to it.

I came to be involved in this ministry in an unusual and striking way, a way that was to mark me throughout the world as one with considerable experience in the area of alien entities.

I was always willing to do anything for God. I did not seek to specialize in any form of ministry. Only as God opened doors did I walk through those doors. Only as I saw the work of God being hampered did I move into this area which was actually not of my own choosing at all.

But since I have been in this ministry for so long, as to such an extent, I feel it would be beneficial to you if I explained how it came about, how I discovered alien entities in human beings.

The First Discovery in Indonesia

I grew up in what was called Christian America. I had never witnessed a person manifesting an alien entity. According to the way I was taught in the church and society to which my family and I belonged, if a person became ill physically we prayed for him to be healed. If he went crazy, we just put him in the insane asylum. No problem at all, he was just put away. We thought that was the only thing we could do, since we couldn't really understand what he was saying anyway.

We never realized that a person could be oppressed of the devil and could be set free by the same kind of prayer as if he had appendicitis. Somehow the two never were related in our minds.

When I began to preach, I spiritualized everything. I said, "Demon power reveals the fury of sin." I said, "Palsy in the Bible reveals the helplessness of sin." Then I said, "If you have leprosy, it will show you how sin eats away your life, that you are helpless before the power of sin."

I did so because that was just the way I was taught. It was only when I went overseas to engage in missionary evangelism that the awakening came. It had not been part of my training, my religious thinking, or my personal experience to give consideration to a human person being demon possessed in these modern times.

I was ministering with Howard Carter in revival and teaching crusades across the island of Java in Indonesia. In a large church a girl of about 12 years of age began to slither back and forth across the altar area of the church during the song service and prelimi-naries. She would stick out her tongue. Her eyes became like a serpent's eyes and green froth came out of her mouth. This was a totally new experience for me.

I thought to myself, "I'm sure the pastor will take care of this situation."

But he didn't. Neither the pastor nor the church officials nor the ushers paid her any attention what-soever. For a full 45 or 50 minutes she went back and forth in front of the altar grinning, always looking at the platform. When she would crawl one way, she would face the platform. Then when she crawled back, she would turn her head around to keep facing the platform. It seemed to be the center of her attention.

I prayed silently, "Lord, just save souls."

But God said, "I can't. You've got that problem down there."

"Well," I said, "You take care of it."

God answered back, "That's *your* problem."

I had never had such a problem in my life. I had no idea what to do nor how to do it. I just sat there in utter hurt and confusion for the whole 50 minutes, wishing somebody would take care of the situation, but nobody did a thing about it.

I was a foreigner there. That was the first time I had ever been in that church. I didn't speak their language.

I was seated about four or five steps back from the pulpit on the large platform. When I was introduced, I walked to the pulpit to speak. But rather than greeting the people by saying, "Good evening. How are you?", I leaned over the pulpit and ordered, "Get up off that floor!" The interpreter, scared, never opened his mouth.

Now I did not know one word of Javanese, and the girl didn't speak any English. But the devil understood it. That poor little girl wiped the green foam off her face, backed up and sat on the pew. She didn't sit there like a human. She sat there like a zombie and just stared at me without moving a muscle all the time I was preaching. When I got through with my sermon, I leaned back over the pulpit again and I said, "Now, come out of her!"

I'd never heard anyone do that before. I just did it. And I spoke loudly too. I said it so loud, you could have heard me down the street. (I haven't decided yet why it takes loudness, except that the devil is dull of hearing. If you don't get his attention, you don't get anything.)

I never did get close to the girl. But as soon as I spoke, immediately the Spirit of the Lord came upon her. Her eyes came back into focus. Her face that had been contorted was changed. Her body became relaxed, and she smiled.

My interpreter was listening, and he interpreted to me what the girl said. She turned to the person sitting next to her and asked, "Where am I? And what am I doing here?" She had been so full of Satan that she didn't even know where she was or how she had gotten there. By two strikes of the Holy Spirit she was set free.

Hundreds of people got saved that evening. They just came flocking down all the aisles. When that girl was set free, they began to come from everywhere to receive the Lord Jesus Christ.

After the service, I slipped back to my room. I was traveling with Howard Carter, the president of a Bible college in London and a great man of God. I told him, "Brother Carter, you may not want to travel with me anymore."

"Why is that?" he asked.

I explained to him what had happened and what I had done. "I screamed at her," I told him. "She got set free. But I have never seen anything like that in church before."

Brother Carter just smiled and remarked, "It sounds all right to me."

Well, it may have sounded all right to him, but I was not at all sure it was all right with me. I had never seen such a thing in my life.

Because of that experience, I was a little hesitant to go out on my own again for a while, so Brother Carter and I decided that perhaps we should stay together if possible. In those countries we had so many people begging for us to come that we would often split up. He was a teacher and I was an evangelist so he would be in one place ministering and I would be in another. But sure enough, it happened again, the next time I went out alone to preach.

"You Have a Black Angel"

In less than ten days' time I was in another service in Java. I entered the church with my interpreter. The building was packed with people who had come to see the visiting preacher from America. The church was so full that extra chairs had to be put in the aisles. The interpreter and I made our way slowly through the crowd toward the platform.

About one third of the way down the aisle, someone grabbed hold of my coat sleeve and wouldn't let go. I shook my arm to no effect. I looked around, and a Javanese woman had clinched my coat. I pulled, but she held tight. I didn't know what to do since I was a stranger there.

I leaned over toward her and she grinned a strange smile, her eyes darting like serpent fangs. She said in English, "You have a black angel in you, and I have a white angel in me." She ended her sentence with a hideous giggle.

The Spirit of the Lord rose up within me. I became angry. Suddenly I laid hands on her head and cried: "That is a lie! You have the devil in you and I have Jesus Christ within me!"

With a special anointing from God, I said in a firm voice, "Come out of her, you foul and unclean spirit!"

Instantly she released my coat. Her contorted face changed expression. She smiled and her eyes softened.

I asked her, "How long have you been possessed?"

She replied, "Fifteen years ago I went to a witch doctor with some domestic troubles. That is when the spirit possessed me. I have been abnormal ever since. But when you commanded that evil spirit to come out, it left me. It is gone now."

We had a great church service that night. The power of the Lord had come. I didn't have to preach much. I just exhorted the people for a few minutes, and again the crowds came rushing down to give their hearts to God.

The Ministry Unfolds

So then I began to put things together. If you set people free from the devil's power, all kinds of people get saved. The Lord began to whisper to me, "If you can bind the strong man, you can spoil his house."

All the sinners are the devil's prey. When you bind him first, even before you preach, then you can get the prey. You can get the ones he has been holding captive in his prison house. You jar his gates loose and you get his prey, when you first set the people free.

We went through the whole island of Java. There were over 50 million people there at that time. (There might be from 70 to 100 million by now.) We found that in almost every city this same situation occurred; and when it did, God provided a deliverance that everybody in the service could witness and respond to.

Howard Carter and I would discuss these incidents. Almost every time they took place, it would be at a time when he wouldn't be there with me. I began to think the devil was manipulating things to catch him not there to try to pick on me because I was young and new at this business. Howard Carter was over twice my age.

We went all through the Orient. This sort of thing happened so much I named it the Oriental disease. I thought to myself, "Man, these people over here have it bad." After we had been all through the Orient, up through China, Japan and Korea, we came back across Siberia and Russia.

When we got to Europe, I thought I had left all that kind of thing behind. I was sure I wouldn't find it in modern, sophisticated Europe. We hadn't been in Europe but a week, until again Brother Carter and I found ourselves separated from each other. We were each preaching in different places for the sake of the people.

In one of my services, a woman of about 30 years of age sat on the front row of the auditorium. All through the service, from the very beginning, she would say "hallelujah!" in a strained and peculiar voice. It sounded awful. She said it about every minute.

I was wondering why somebody didn't stop her, or choke her, or something because what she was doing wasn't normal. It wasn't natural. And it certainly wasn't spiritual. Again I thought, "I'm sure the pastor will take care of this situation." But no, he looked up at the ceiling and totally ignored her.

I thought, "Surely the ushers will come down here and stop all this." But it went right on, through the whole meeting.

I kept thinking, "God, stop that woman."

He said to me, "I can't. You stop her."

Finally, after almost an hour of preliminaries it was my time to preach. I walked up to the platform with my interpreter. While I was sitting on the platform,

I didn't know what I was going to do. But when I got to the pulpit, I just leaned over and said to the lady, "And, you, shut up!" The interpreter never said a word. He just stood there. And she didn't shut up. She started barking like a dog. I thought, "I could have done better with the hallelujahs!" There is such a thing as making a condition worse.

Suddenly down the aisles came the ushers. That made me angry. They didn't do a thing when she was yelling hallelujah like a donkey. But when she started to bark like a dog, they didn't like the barking. One was just as bad as the other to me.

I grabbed my interpreter and told him, "You tell them I said to sit down." They hadn't come to help, and I didn't want them down there. So they went back to their places and the lady was still barking.

I commanded that spirit in her, "Come out of her!" God set her free instantly. She smiled. She didn't bark and she didn't say the strange hallelujah, either. The Spirit of the Lord came upon her. But the sweet thing is, the Spirit of the Lord came upon the whole place. That night, many people were saved.

Later I told Brother Carter, "I'll tell you, Brother Carter, that Oriental disease has made it to Europe. It's bad. A woman said hallelujah like an animal. Then she barked like a dog."

I said, "From the platform, without touching her, I set her free. And she is free."

Brother Carter replied, "Well, God is going to use you that way."

"I hope not," I told him. "I want to be a nice, clean little evangelist."

In Europe

We had problems throughout France. There were many possessed people there. Then through Holland, Belgium, Norway, and Sweden, the same situation. England was one of the foremost places. So many people there needed help to send forth spirits out of them.

I was learning about alien entities in every country we visited. But I didn't want to learn. I didn't want to get involved in it, and I wasn't preaching about it. I wasn't creating the atmosphere. It was just there.

Most of the time when it happened I couldn't preach without doing something about it. I had to take care of it or I couldn't speak to the people. This spirit manifestation was blocking the message, and so I had to do something.

In America

After months and months, we came across the Atlantic Ocean, back home. I said to Brother Carter, "I'll tell you one thing, those people in the Orient and those in Europe have a bad disease. But we don't have it in America. I've lived there all my life and I haven't seen any."

So we got back to the States. My brother, Huston Sumrall, was a pastor of a church in the St. Louis area. I went to see him. After I had preached for him, I preached for some other churches around St. Louis. In one city, after preaching on Sunday morning, I went out with the pastor to have lunch in a restaurant.

After lunch the pastor asked, "Would you go with me to pray for one of my members?" I really didn't want to go. But I said, "Well, I guess so."

We drove to a humble little midwestern home, a two-bedroom white frame house with a swing on the front porch. We walked up on the porch, and the pastor opened the door.

Inside I saw a young man about 26 or 27 years old. His mother was kneeling down beside his chair saying, "Son, speak to me. Speak to Mama." She had a platter in one hand and a spoon in the other. It was obvious that she had just fed him.

As it turned out, this young man had gone to a spiritist seance six months before. He had gone just for "kicks," thinking it would be fun to talk to the dead and feel eerie spirits in the shadows. To him it was just a game. But the next morning he was found lying on his mother's front porch. He had no shirt on, scratches all over his back, and he could not speak. When I arrived he had not said a word in six months.

He also became strange in his body movements. You could put his arm out and he would leave it there for hours in the same position. He did not seem to get tired. If you wanted it moved, you would have to move it yourself.

He could eat if food was placed in his mouth, so his mother fed him like a baby. He slept all right when he was put to bed, but he had to be stretched out because he would remain in the same position he was placed in all night long.

The mother didn't know what had happened to cause this state to come on her son. All she knew was that she found him on the front porch in a coma. When she was finally able to get him inside, he couldn't move his body or say a word. The family had asked for prayer so the pastor had asked me to go with him. The pastor didn't tell me what the problem was, he just asked me to go with him to pray for one of his church families.

As we walked in the front door, we could hear the mother begging her son to speak to her. Just then I saw the strangest little curve at the edge of his mouth. It was a satanic grin, the grin of victory. It was the devil's way of saying, "I've got you!" A devilish little smirk that I could see from across the room.

Suddenly I leaped across that room like a panther. I grabbed that young man on both sides of his head, and I said, "You unclean spirit, you hear my voice. Come out! You speak to your mother and you hurry!"

The young man said, "Mother, I'm so sorry I've caused all this trouble for you. I promise never to do it again." In our presence he told her how he had gotten messed up in a spiritist seance when he had let himself be put under a spell. He didn't know what was going on until he was set free from that demonic possession.

So, beginning with that experience I discovered that the same thing I had encountered in Asia and in Europe was also going on right here in this country. From that time to this, I have seen literally thousands of people set free from the devil's power in dozens of nations throughout the world. I have already described some of these instances in this book.

How It Happens

So that is how I became involved in the ministry of deliverance from demon oppression and demon possession. I never sought such a ministry; it was thrust upon me. I have never done any of this to promote myself, to receive anything for myself, nor to cause others to think well of me. In every instance, it was almost a case of desperation. I had to lean heavily upon God and give Him all the glory. He is worthy of all the glory, because He is the One Who does it.

I never look or seek for those who need deliverance. When God sends them to me, I deal with them in sincerity and truth. Many are set free. At times I do not see a visible change, but if the person wishes to and will obey instructions, I will keep ministering to him.

You too can have victory, strength and power. God will lead you, just as He has led me and many others. But He never leads any two persons in exactly the same way. He will lead you individually and personally, and you will be unique in the way and the manner in which you set others free.

17

Biblical Examples of Possession by Alien Entities

In this study, we are dealing with the most important subject on successful Christian living that can be taught from the Word of God. Until a Christian knows how to defeat the enemy, he cannot be a successful and victorious soldier of the Cross. The key to being a victorious soldier lies in knowing the enemy.

In analyzing our enemy, we are not exalting him in any form or fashion. On the contrary, we are downgrading and destroying him. The more we know about him and his ways, the better able we are to defeat him. **...for we are not ignorant of his devices** (2 Cor. 2:11).

The Man With 2,000 Entities

And he asked him, What is thy name? And he answered, saying, My name is Legion: for we are many.

Mark 5:9

The demoniac of Gadara seems to hold first place in the number of alien entities to possess one person. His people in Gadara believed him to be possessed. The local people tried to assist him, but the strange man was normal one moment and wild the next. The populace sought to tie him down and bind him, for his own safety as well as theirs, but they could not hold him. He would tear off his clothes and spend time wandering around in the cemeteries, screaming and cutting himself with sharp stones. There seemed no hope for him.

Then Jesus arrived in that land. Screaming in fury, the wild man ran out to meet Him. He had never met the Master before, only helpless human sinners. He suddenly realized he had come face to face with One stronger than he. He recognized Jesus as his authority.

The man himself did not speak. But the angry and now fearful spirit within him cried out, **What have I to do with thee, Jesus, thou Son of the most high God?...torment me not** (v. 7).

Jesus caused the unclean and violent spirit to confess his identity: **...My name is Legion: for we are many** (v. 9). In the Roman army a legion was a unit of more than 2,000 soldiers. The demoniac seems to be the most possessed person on record.

This reveals to us something very remarkable. A spirit does not occupy physical space within a human. A person can have many spirits within him, manifesting themselves through him, yet not taking up any part of the organic being inside him. Here was a man who had at least 2,000 evil spirits within him. Yet there was plenty of room for more.

Jesus spoke to the spirit positively and with authority: **...Come out of the man, thou unclean spirit** (v. 8). Immediately the possessed man was set free. The Bible says that he sat at the feet of Jesus, **...clothed, and in his right mind...**(v. 15).

Then the man said to Jesus, "Lord, I want to go with You and be a disciple." But Jesus saw the wisdom of his going back to his own people, rather than following Him off somewhere else: **Howbeit Jesus suffered him not, but saith unto him, Go home to thy friends, and tell them how great things the Lord hath done for thee, and hath had compassion on thee** (v. 19).

When God does something great for you, it is so easy to want to run off some place to tell about it. It is better to tell your family, friends and neighbors first, those who are the most familiar with you and your need. They are better able to understand and appreciate "how great things the Lord hath done for thee."

It is a stronger thing to set the house in order where you are. So Jesus sent the man back to his own home and to his friends: **And he departed, and began to publish in Decapolis how great things Jesus had done for him: and all men did marvel** (v. 20).

Today, many men, women, boys and girls are tormented by alien entities. The medical world is frustrated before them. The domestic world misjudges them. They are hurt, lonely, and many have lost hope.

Jesus is passing their way! They can receive deliverance! Just like the man of Gadara.

Mary Magdalene Had Seven Entities

Now when Jesus was risen early the first day of the week, he appeared first to Mary Magdalene, out of whom he had cast seven devils.

Mark 16:9

The next story is similar, but the person involved is a woman.

Though not to belabor this point, I do want to mention that women are very prominent in the area of witchcraft and the occult. Some time ago I asked a witch doctor in Africa if there were witch doctors active in this modern age.

"Yes," he replied.

"Are there more male or female witch doctors?" I inquired.

He answered, "The witch doctors are overwhelmingly female, not male."

"Why is that?" I asked.

"It is easier for a woman to touch spiritual forces. They can release themselves to the spirits so much easier."

I recently read in a secular magazine that in Philadelphia alone there are 3,000 witches and most of them are women. Why? I only have one possible explanation. The devil hates Eve because she produced the Messiah Who stepped on his head. He is still angry about that and wants to hurt her and destroy her descendants in every way he can.

Also on the side of the Lord Jesus, it might be said that those who received Him best and remained most loyal to Him in His earthly lifetime were women. One of these ladies is the subject of our story, Mary Magdalene, a most remarkable woman of history.

Mary had a bad start and fell off the bottom rung of the social ladder early in life. Then she met the most wonderful person in all history, Jesus of Nazareth.

The name *Mary* is derived from the Old Testament name *Miriam* and means rebellion. There were at least six Marys mentioned in the New Testament.

Here are seven remarkable aspects of the life of this Mary:

1. She was the infamous Mary of Magdala.

Mary was from the city of Magdala on the Sea of Galilee. There are only ruins there today. She was delivered from a very sinful life. We know she was delivered and transformed into a wonderful, pure woman, and became a leader of women.

2. Jesus found Mary and cast seven devils out of her.

> And it came to pass afterward, that he went throughout every city and village, preaching and shewing the glad tidings of the kingdom of God: and the twelve were with him.
>
> And certain women, which had been healed of evil spirits and infirmities, Mary called Magdalene, out of whom went seven devils....
>
> Luke 8:1,2

These are possibly the kinds of entities which tormented Mary. The Bible says there were seven evil spirits in her:

1) **Rebellion, anger**
2) **Lust, adultery, harlotry**
3) **Hate, murder**
4) **Pride**
5) **Lying**
6) **Stealing**
7) **Witchcraft**

Mary was also sick. Perhaps this is why she sought out Jesus. The Word says she was among those women who had been healed of "evil spirits and infirmities."

3. Mary left her old life and supported Jesus' ministry.

> And certain women, which had been healed of evil spirits and infirmities, Mary called Magdalene, out of whom went seven devils,
>
> And Joanna the wife of Chuza Herod's steward, and Susanna, and many others, which ministered unto him of their substance.
>
> Luke 8:2,3

Mary Magdalene chose to be close to the One Who had changed her world. She stuck with Him from the day of her deliverance until the very end.

4. Mary followed Jesus even to the cross.

> Now there stood by the cross of Jesus his mother, and his mother's sister, Mary the wife of Cleophas, and Mary Magdalene.
>
> John 19:25

> And many women were there beholding afar off, which followed Jesus from Galilee, ministering unto him:
>
> Among which was Mary Magdalene, and Mary the mother of James and Joses, and the mother of Zebedee's children.
>
> Matthew 27:55,56

5. Mary was the first one to the tomb.

> The first day of the week cometh Mary Magdalene early, when it was yet dark, unto the sepulchre, and seeth the stone taken away from the sepulchre.
>
> John 20:1

Mary's heart of love demanded this action.

> And when the sabbath was past, Mary Magdalene, and Mary the mother of James, and Salome, had bought sweet spices, that they might come and anoint him.
>
> Mark 16:1

Mary came to anoint the body of Jesus. Just as she had ministered to Him in life, so now she came to minister to her Lord after His death and burial.

> And entering into the sepulchre, they saw a young man sitting on the right side, clothed in a long white garment; and they were affrighted.
>
> And he saith unto them, Be not affrighted: Ye seek Jesus of Nazareth, which was crucified: he is risen; he is not here: behold the place where they laid him.
>
> But go your way, tell his disciples and Peter that he goeth before you into Galilee: there shall ye see him, as he said unto you.
>
> Mark 16:5-7

Mary talked with an angel and broadcast the news of the empty tomb.

> Then she runneth, and cometh to Simon Peter, and to the other disciple, whom Jesus loved....
>
> John 20:2

6. Mary was the first to see the risen Lord.

> Now when Jesus was risen early the first day of the week, he appeared first to Mary Magdalene, out of whom he had cast seven devils.
>
> Mark 16:9

> Jesus saith unto her, Mary. She turned herself, and saith unto him, Rabboni; which is to say, Master.
>
> John 20:16

7. Mary was the first evangelist of the Resurrection.

> Mary Magdalene came and told the disciples that she had seen the Lord, and that he had spoken these things unto her.
>
> John 20:18

I accentuate this truth for one purpose. No matter how deeply into demon possession a person has gone, how many entities may have been within him (or her), he (or she) can still love and serve God after deliverance.

Mary Magdalene is evidence of that truth.

The Fortune Teller With an Alien Entity

> And it came to pass, as we went to prayer, a certain damsel possessed with a spirit of divination met us, which brought her masters much gain by soothsaying.
>
> Acts 16:16

This is the case of another woman. She was involved in witchcraft. According to the Bible, she "brought her masters much gain by soothsaying."

It is no wonder people want to try to convince us they can foretell the future. There is much financial gain involved in fortune telling, much more than most of us would ever imagine. These people don't care anything about your future; all they care about is the gain in it for themselves.

Almost from the beginning of time, certain persons have felt that they possess information beyond the normal human mind. They invariably seek to influence leaders in business and politics. When Joseph arrived in Egypt, Pharaoh had magicians: **And it came to pass in the morning that his** (Pharaoh's) **spirit was troubled; and he sent and called for all the magicians of Egypt, and all the wise men thereof: and Pharaoh told them his dream; but there was none that could interpret them unto Pharaoh** (Gen. 41:8). This was 1,700 years before the time of Christ.

When Moses confronted a different pharaoh some 400 years later, he still had his wise men, magicians, and sorcerers who used enchantments to try to match the power of Jehovah:

> **And Moses and Aaron went in unto Pharaoh, and they did so as the LORD had commanded: and Aaron cast down his rod before Pharaoh, and before his servants, and it became a serpent.**
>
> **Then Pharaoh also called the wise men and the sorcerers: now the magicians of Egypt, they also did in like manner with their enchantments....**
>
> **...and Pharaoh's heart was hardened, neither did he hearken unto them; as the LORD had said.**
>
> **Exodus 7:10,11,22**

This teaches us one thing. While Joseph was alive, the Egyptians would take his blessing, but not his God. They never stopped worshipping the devil.

By the time the first world empire of Babylon was flourishing between the Tigris and Euphrates rivers, demon power had risen to eminence. Magicians and wizards were on the payroll of Nebuchadnezzar, the emperor.

The king commanded his magicians, astrologers, sorcerers and the Chaldeans to reveal to him a forgotten dream he had had: **Then the king commanded to call the magicians, and the astrologers, and the sorcerers, and the Chaldeans, for to shew the king his dreams. So they came and stood before the king** (Dan. 2:2).

But even the devil could not help his slaves. The king threatened to cut them to pieces and make their homes a dunghill if they failed to tell him the dream and its interpretation: **The king answered and said to the Chaldeans, The thing is gone from me: if ye will not make known unto me the dream, with the interpretation thereof, ye shall be cut in pieces, and your houses shall be made a dunghill** (v. 5).

It was Daniel who saved their necks by revealing to the king the dream of the giant image of gold, silver, brass, iron and clay, representing the history of Gentile empires. (Dan. 2:14-45.)

God's Word about Fortune Telling

When thou art come into the land which the LORD thy God giveth thee, thou shalt not learn to do after the abominations of those nations.

There shall not be found among you any one that maketh his son or his daughter to pass through the fire, or that useth divination, or an observer of times, or an enchanter, or a witch,

Or a charmer, or a consulter with familiar spirits, or a wizard, or a necromancer.

For all that do these things are an abomination unto the LORD: and because of these abominations the LORD thy God doth drive them out from before thee.

Thou shalt be perfect with the LORD thy God.

> **For these nations, which thou shalt possess, hearkened unto observers of times, and unto diviners: but as for thee the LORD thy God hath not suffered thee so to do.**
>
> **Deuteronomy 18:9-14**

You and I are not the first to come up against demon power, nor was Jesus. From the earliest times the devil has been coming to possess people and cause them to follow him. He wants to lead them away from the living God so they will think they can find another way to heaven. His ultimate plan and purpose is the destruction of mankind.

But each time, God has given His servants authority, strength and power so they can re-direct the course of mankind—take them back to God so they can be victorious.

We are not losers! I wish we could get that truth through to the mind and spirit of the Church of Jesus Christ.

Every time there has been an earthly empire, the devil has tried to take that empire. I have heard that there are more soothsayers, fortune tellers, and people who read crystal balls, in Washington, D.C., our national capital, than possibly any other city on earth.

There are mediums today who are possessed by the alien entity of fortune telling and who practice their devilish art through one of the following means:

1. **Astrology**
2. **Crystal ball gazing**
3. **Card reading**
4. **Palm reading**

5. Seances

When the first of the year rolls around, our magazines are full of what these people are predicting for the coming year. Come December, no mention is ever made of the 9/10's of their predictions which never came true. No newspaper ever carries that news.

When God speaks, He is not a liar. When the devil speaks, you can't believe a word he says because he doesn't even know what he is talking about. He is only guessing. Only God knows the future. Only God can speak the future. God will speak that future through His Church, not through demon power.

We have the greatest onslaught of demonic forces functioning against our society today than ever before in history. There are actually people in this nation who belong to what they call "Satan's Church." There is even evidence that in the United States of America, in our lifetime, people have actually offered human sacrifices to the devil!

We Christians are needed in the world more today than ever before. We are the marching army of the Lord Jesus Christ. What upsets me more than anything is the fact that many churches, many pastors, many Christians would not dare come against the devil as a person. Or come against his kingdom. Or come against a possessed person and command that he be set free.

If the devil was working in Egypt, if he was working in Babylon, then in Persia, in the mythologies of Ancient Greece and Rome, he hasn't gone out of business nor stopped working in high places today.

But with the knowledge of God within us, the anointing of God upon us, and the power of God behind us, we can set humanity free.

18

Pertinent Inquiries Regarding Alien Entities

I am asked more questions about the world of demonic influence than about any other subject. In this chapter I will attempt to briefly answer some of these questions, although I could write a separate chapter on each of them.

1. How many alien entities are there?

Evidently, from what the Apostle John said in Revelation 12:4, when Lucifer was cast out of heaven he brought down with him one third of the angelic host: **And his tail drew the third part of the stars of heaven, and did cast them to the earth: and the dragon stood before the woman which was ready to be delivered, for to devour her child as soon as it was born.**

This must have been the group over which Satan presided. He had enough power of persuasion to convince them that he could do more for them than the One Who created them.

Lucifer and his followers had worked together for eternity before their rebellion. There was no history for them to refer to, so they obviously believed him and followed him into rebellion against the Most High God.

Their number has never been divulged. There could well be millions or even billions of fallen angels referred to as alien entities in this lesson.

2. Can an alien entity attack a Christian?

Yes. Satan and his angels do have the liberty to entice, to attract away from God, to tempt a believer in Christ. This is not surprising because Satan tempted Eve by his lies in the Garden of Eden. She did not have to believe the devil's lies. Her force of will power yielded to her eyes, her ears, her taste. She deliberately decided against God. It was a conscious act of her volition, a responsible decision.

In Matthew 4, we read that Satan even tempted Jesus Christ. If he will attack God's very own Son, certainly he will attack the believer.

3. Are alien entities more active in one nation than in another?

Yes. In my travels in more than 100 nations of the world, I have found that certain lands are more controlled by alien entities than others. For example, India, Haiti, and Tibet are places where extreme control by demonic forces can be witnessed.

You will remember from the book of Genesis that the cities of Sodom and Gomorrah were under an especially strong control of Satan: **And the LORD said, ...the cry of Sodom and Gomorrah is great, and...their sin is very grievous** (Gen. 18:20).

Babylon is referred to in the Bible as the habitation of devils: **And he cried mightily with a strong voice, saying, Babylon the great is fallen, is fallen,**

and is become the habitation of devils, and the hold of every foul spirit, and a cage of every unclean and hateful bird (Rev. 18:2). A hold is a dwelling place, a reserved place, a place of hiding where a person (or spirit) can go for security. I can assure you that there are areas on earth where Satan has more control, more authority, and does more damage than in other places.

Where there is singing and rejoicing, where the Word of God is read and proclaimed, where people live clean lives, the devil has a hard time gaining a foothold. But in places where sin abounds, Satan develops a stronghold.

There are geographical areas—nations, regions, cities—which are more active with demon power than others.

4. Can a demon-possessed person be set free against his will?

No, he cannot. I have observed this all over the world. Any deliverance of a person who does not want to be free will be temporary at best. If set free against his will, the person will be possessed again as soon as the demon decides to come back into him.

In Luke 11:24-26 Jesus tells us:

> **When the unclean spirit is gone out of a man, he walketh through dry places, seeking rest; and finding none, he saith, I will return unto my house whence I came out.**
>
> **And when he cometh, he findeth it swept and garnished.**
>
> **Then goeth he, and taketh to him seven other spirits more wicked than himself; and they enter in,**

and dwell there: and the last state of that man is worse than the first.

If a person does not really want to be free of demon control, he will soon allow the spirit to re-enter. This time, there will be more spirits and the person's condition will be worse than at the beginning.

However, if a person is completely insane, like the demoniac of Gadara, you can set him free and then ask him if he would like to stay free. If he says yes, then he can remain free forever. But if he says no, he will soon allow himself to be re-possessed by the devil.

5. Is possession by alien entities constant or sporadic?

When a person is possessed, he is possessed. But the manifestation of that possession might be sporadic. The possession itself is constant and continuing, though there may not necessarily be any manifestation of it at any particular moment.

The spirit possessing a person can manifest itself at various times. For example, the witch doctor from Brazil had some spirits in him which only manifested themselves one time a year. Other people may have demonic spirits which manifest themselves every day.

The demoniac of Gadara had become an uncontrollable wild man living in a cemetery and cutting himself with stones. When Jesus came, the demoniac screamed out, "I know You! Have You come to torment me before my time?" But the possessed man in the synagogue was comfortable at church among other people. Yet both were possessed of demons.

The Buddhist priest in Yunnan, Southwest China, told me that the large idol of Buddha was only a symbol until he offered incense, burnt candles, presented gifts of food, and prostrated himself before it. Then the spirit of the idol came and manifested itself to the worshipper.

Thus, demon possession is a state of being, not a particular action, although the alien entity will usually manifest itself in one way or another.

6. How many demons can one person have?

It can vary from one to thousands. Many people in the Bible were plagued with only one alien entity. In Mark 9:25 we read: **When Jesus saw that the people came running together, he rebuked the foul spirit, saying unto him, Thou dumb and deaf spirit, I charge thee, come out of him, and enter no more into him.** This person was possessed of one spirit which manifested itself in two ways, deafness and dumbness.

In Luke 11:26 we read of a person with eight alien entities living in him: **Then goeth he, and taketh to him seven other spirits more wicked than himself; and they enter in, and dwell there: and the last state of that man is worse than the first.**

The demoniac of Gadara was controlled by a legion of (at least two thousand) demons: **And Jesus asked him, saying, What is thy name? And he said, Legion: because many devils were entered into him** (Luke 8:30).

7. Can demons be inherited?

Yes. In Java I met a man who had seven spirits which manifested through him. He had "willed" these spirits to his teenaged son. The lad was happy to receive these alien entities and was eager for them to come into him at his father's death.

8. Can a person be possessed and not know it?

Yes. Many people have demonic problems which they do not recognize. Usually these people realize that they have a problem but do not understand exactly what it is. Many times they do not even believe in the reality of demons.

This is one of Satan's greatest deceptions.

An example of a time when even the disciples were under the influence of spirits which they did not recognize is found in Luke 9:55: **But he (Jesus) turned, and rebuked them, and said, Ye know not what manner of spirit ye are of.**

In Matthew 16:23 Jesus declares that Satan is working as an alien influence through Peter without the apostle's knowledge: **But he (Jesus) turned, and said unto Peter, Get thee behind me, Satan: thou art an offence unto me: for thou savourest not the things that be of God, but those that be of men.**

9. Can animals be possessed?

Yes. The classic Biblical example is Satan's entering into the serpent: **Now the serpent was more subtil than any beast of the field which the Lord God had made. And he said unto the woman, Yea, hath God said, Ye shall not eat of every tree of the garden?** (Gen. 3:1).

In the New Testament, we read of spirits entering into pigs: **Then went the devils out of the man,**

and entered into the swine: and the herd ran violently down a steep place into the lake, and were choked (Luke 8:33).

Today we have many examples of dogs, horses, and other animals suddenly going mad. Many times, they injure themselves or people, even sometimes becoming man-killers, and must be destroyed. This sudden rush of violence indicates the presence of an alien entity.

10. Can a Christian be cursed by demons?

Only if he allows it. According to the Bible, every Christian has the right and power to resist the devil and his attacks:

> **Submit yourselves therefore to God. Resist the devil, and he will flee from you.**
>
> James 4:7

> **Above all, taking the shield of faith, wherewith ye shall be able to quench all the fiery darts of the wicked.**
>
> Ephesians 6:16

> **No weapon that is formed against thee shall prosper; and every tongue that shall rise against thee in judgment thou shalt condemn. This is the heritage of the servants of the LORD, and their righteousness is of me, saith the LORD.**
>
> Isaiah 54:17

> **So shall they fear the name of the Lord from the west, and his glory from the rising of the sun. When the enemy shall come in like a flood, the Spirit of the Lord shall lift up a standard against him.**
>
> Isaiah 59:19

If you will study the Word of God, you will find that you are absolutely secure in Jesus. He that is in you is greater than he that is in the world. (1 John 4:4.) If you resist the devil, he will flee from you. (James 4:7.) How could you be in the Lord's army if you were afraid that the other army could get inside of you? You couldn't win any battles that way. That idea is simply the devil's way of trying to put fear into people's hearts.

You would be amazed at the number of people who come to me saying that they are under a curse. I ask them if they are Christian and they say they are. I then tell them that one or the other of their statements is wrong. Either they are not Christian, or they are not under a curse.

Galatians 3:13,14 tells us that **Christ hath redeemed us from the curse..., being made a curse for us...That the blessing of Abraham might come on the Gentiles** (us) **through Jesus Christ....** If we have been redeemed from the curse, if we are blessed of God, then the devil cannot curse us: **How shall I curse, whom God hath not cursed? or how shall I defy, whom the Lord hath not defied?** (Num. 23:8).

11. Are there always physical manifestations when alien entities leave?

Many times there are physical manifestations: **And the spirit cried, and rent him sore, and came out of him, and he was as one dead; insomuch that many said, He is dead** (Mark 9:26).

However, this is not always the case. I have often seen people set free when there was no physical manifestation. I sensed the person's release in my spirit and knew that the alien entity was gone. Paul describes this spiritual witness in Romans 8:15,16:

> **For ye have not received the spirit of bondage again to fear; but ye have received the Spirit of adoption, whereby we cry, Abba, Father.**
>
> **The Spirit itself beareth witness with our spirit, that we are the children of God.**

12. Can a house be possessed of demons?

Yes, alien entities prefer to possess human beings, but they will often live in buildings. I have witnessed this phenomenon in pagan temples around the world. I have also seen it in private dwellings. Many times these are houses in which a violent crime or some occult practice has taken place.

Earlier in this book I described how I once visited in a home in Denver and how a spirit appeared to me in my bedroom during the night. The family who owned the house did not know the tragic story of the house, yet they confirmed that there had been strange occurrences in it, especially in that one bedroom. Later investigation proved that a suicide had taken place in the house and that it had happened in that very room.

13. Was Jesus tempted by alien entities?

In Matthew 4:3,6,9 we read in detail of a three-pronged attack upon Jesus by Satan:

> **And when the tempter came to him, he said, If thou be the Son of God, command that these stones be made bread...**
>
> **And saith unto him, If thou be the Son of God, cast thyself down: for it is written, He shall give his angels charge concerning thee: and in their hands they shall bear thee up, lest at any time thou dash thy foot against a stone...**

And saith unto him, All these things will I give thee, if thou wilt fall down and worship me.

This was the great temptation of Jesus by Satan. However, Jesus was under constant attack by alien entities. In almost every place He ministered, there were demonic manifestations and attacks. Jesus always met, encountered and conquered them.

In Acts 10:38 we read: **How God anointed Jesus of Nazareth with the Holy Ghost and with power: who went about doing good, and healing all that were oppressed of the devil; for God was with him.**

Hebrews 4:13 tells us: **Neither is there any creature that is not manifest in his sight: but all things are naked and opened unto the eyes of him with whom we have to do.**

14. Are there religious entities?

Yes. Actually, the religious entities are often the most difficult to deal with. It was the scribes and the Pharisees along with the high priest himself who gave Jesus the most trouble in His earthly ministry.

Then gathered the chief priests and the Pharisees a council, and said, What do we? for this man doeth many miracles...

Then from that day forth they took counsel together for to put him to death.

John 11:47,53

John warns us that many spirits will work in the area of false religion.

Beloved, believe not every spirit, but try the spirits whether they are of God: because many false prophets are gone out into the world.

> Hereby know ye the Spirit of God: Every spirit
> that confesseth that Jesus Christ is come in the flesh
> is of God:

> And every spirit that confesseth not that Jesus
> Christ is come in the flesh is not of God: and this is
> that spirit of antichrist, whereof ye have heard that
> it should come; and even now already is it in the
> world.

> 1 John 4:1-3

Paul confirms this same revelation in 1 Timothy
4:1-3:

> Now the Spirit speaketh expressly, that in the lat-
> ter times some shall depart from the faith, giving heed
> to seducing spirits, and doctrines of devils;

> Speaking lies in hypocrisy; having their con-
> science seared with a hot iron;

> Forbidding to marry, and commanding to abstain
> from meats, which God hath created to be received
> with thanksgiving of them which believe and know
> the truth.

You must know that false religious spirits will
become more active as we near the end of the present
age:

> For there shall arise false Christs, and false
> prophets, and shall shew great signs and wonders;
> insomuch that, if it were possible, they shall deceive
> the very elect.

> Matthew 24:24

The apex of the power of the false religious spirits
will dwell in the False Prophet. He will use the alien
power to cause the world to follow the Antichrist:

> And after three days and an half the Spirit of life
> from God entered into them, and they stood upon

189

their feet; and great fear fell upon them which saw them.

And they heard a great voice from heaven saying unto them, Come up hither. And they ascended up to heaven in a cloud; and their enemies beheld them.

And the same hour was there a great earthquake, and the tenth part of the city fell, and in the earthquake were slain of men seven thousand: and the remnant were affrighted, and gave glory to the God of heaven.

The second woe is past; and, behold, the third woe cometh quickly.

And the seventh angel sounded; and there were great voices in heaven, saying, The kingdoms of this world are become the kingdoms of our Lord, and of his Christ; and he shall reign for ever and ever.

And the four and twenty elders, which sat before God on their seats, fell upon their faces, and worshipped God,

Saying, We give thee thanks, O Lord God Almighty, which art, and wast, and art to come; because thou hast taken to thee thy great power, and hast reigned.

And the nations were angry, and thy wrath is come, and the time of the dead, that they should be judged, and that thou shouldest give reward unto thy servants the prophets, and to the saints, and them that fear thy name, small and great; and shouldest destroy them which destroy the earth.

Revelation 11:11-18

In these last days in which we live, there is going to be an acceleration of demon power in religion. We see this in our country at this moment in the gurus who have come here from India. They say they have come to teach Americans how to have peace, how to have a mind that is comforted. They are deceiving many.

I recently visited a Buddhist temple in downtown San Francisco, close to Chinatown. One whole wall in the temple was solid gold. As I looked through this gorgeous temple, worth millions of dollars, I looked into a lavish and beautiful theater area. All the seats were plush. Some 300 people were there taking lessons in Buddhism. Every one of those people was an American.

The final struggle of the ages has already begun on the face of this earth today. The final victory which we have just been reading about is apparent. The greatest masterpiece of this struggle will be religious in nature.

The False Prophet will stand beside the Antichrist, and the Bible says that he will bring fire down from heaven in the sight of men. He will cause that idol to speak like a man speaks. All the world will say, "Who is like him?" The greatest deception of all will be a religious deception.

Those of us with spiritual discernment will understand these things when they start to happen. But we must have more and more spiritual discernment in all our churches today. Otherwise, the things which are about to take place in this last generation "shall deceive the very elect." That is why I have been moved by the Holy Spirit of God to write this book: **To open their eyes, and to turn them from darkness to light, and from the power of Satan unto God...** (Acts 26:18). **...to shew unto his servants things which must shortly come to pass...** (Rev. 1:1).

19

Who Can Exorcise an Alien Entity?

And these signs shall follow them that believe; In my name shall they cast out devils....

Mark 16:17

Any believer, any born-again person, anyone who knows the Lord Jesus Christ personally can cast out devils.

In Mark 16:17,18 Jesus tells us that certain signs shall follow those who believe, and the very first one of these signs is the fact that they—*all* of them—shall cast out devils. This ability does not depend upon our own power, strength, faith or name. He said that we shall cast out devils in His Name.

But how does a person come to be able to do that? By coming to Jesus Christ. When can he begin? The moment he is born again.

A person can be born again at this moment, and then immediately walk out on the street and set somebody else free from demon possession. He is on the team already. The instant he comes into the Kingdom of God, he has Kingdom power and authority—*if* he knows it and believes it.

That's the problem. Most Christians do not believe they have that power and authority because they have not been taught that they have it. One of the greatest tragedies of our time is the teaching of unbelief by the

193

clergy. They not only do not teach people that they have power and authority over Satan and his demons, they actually teach the contrary. They say that 2,000 years ago believers had this ability, but not today. According to them, miracles were only given by God to a select few to launch the ministry of the early Church, but that we today are not granted such power and authority.

Nothing could be farther from the truth. We are not eating the leftovers of yesterday's feast. We are right in the middle of today's feast, the best that heaven has to offer. God didn't do any more for those people back then than He will do and is doing for us today. The only difference is, those people back then simply released themselves more to God than we do now. The more we release ourselves to God, the more He does for us and through us.

Other people do not use the power that is theirs as a Christian because they do not think they are "authorized" to do so. They are waiting for their church or denomination or some clerical hierarchy to appoint them to some office or grant them some certain title before they feel they can fulfill this responsibility.

Jesus Christ is the giver of authority. No church or church officer can grant you that power and authority. No one can appoint you. Only those who have the divine authority from Christ Himself can do it. And it begins with the born-again experience of knowing Jesus personally in our heart. From that moment, a person has power over Satan.

The simple truth is, a person can cast out devils when he *knows* he can do it. But how does a person know that he is able to cast out demons?

In considering this question, we must determine who gave the commission, or command, to cast out devils and to whom it was given.

Jesus Gave the Authority

And when he had called unto him his twelve disciples, he gave them power against unclean spirits, to cast them out, and to heal all manner of sickness and all manner of disease.

Matthew 10:1

It was Jesus Christ Who commissioned His first twelve disciples to go and cast out devils.

Later, Jesus apointed seventy others to go and minister. When these seventy apostles returned to Him, they were rejoicing that even the devils were subject unto them by the pronouncing of His name against them: **And the seventy returned again with joy, saying, Lord, even the devils are subject unto us through thy name** (Luke 10:17).

Then just before His ascension into heaven, Jesus instructed His disciples to wait in Jerusalem for a while, telling them: **But ye shall receive power, after that the Holy Ghost is come upon you: and ye shall be witnesses unto me both in Jerusalem, and in all Judaea, and in Samaria, and unto the uttermost part of the earth** (Acts 1:8).

Jesus said that His disciples would receive power after the Holy Ghost had come upon them. Power would be useless if it were not brought against interfering and anti-Christian spirits.

Then in the Great Commission, Jesus authorized and commissioned all believers to carry on His ministry:

> **And he said unto them, Go ye into all the world and preach the gospel to every creature.**
>
> **He that believeth and is baptized shall be saved; but he that believeth not shall be damned.**
>
> **And these signs shall follow them that believe; In my name shall they cast out devils; they shall speak with new tongues;**
>
> **They shall take up serpents; and if they drink any deadly thing, it shall not hurt them; they shall lay hands on the sick, and they shall recover.**
>
> **Mark 16:15-18**

The Lord Jesus specifically said that those who believe would cast out devils. Of course, these are persons who believe and accept the Gospel. They personally know God's power and have become holy vessels unto God. They can accept by faith the sign ministry and therefore exorcise evil spirits.

This simply means that the casting out of spirits does not belong especially to the hierarchy. It does not belong to bishops or men of ecclesiastical position only. It does specifically say that those who exercise faith have this power to relieve those who are tormented by spirits.

I feel it is always best to stick only to what the Bible says about such matters. Church doctrines and church disciplines could lead a person to a non-Biblical position toward those who need divine deliverance.

How Did Jesus Approach Alien Entities?

When Jesus was tempted by Satan in Matthew 4:4, He spoke directly to the devil: **But he answered and** said, It is written, Man shall not live by bread alone, but by every word that proceedeth out of the mouth of God.

Notice that Jesus did not ask His Father to rebuke Satan, but rather He dealt with him personally. In so doing, He was giving us an example of how we are to deal with the adversary.

Jesus recognized the devil's power:

> Again, the devil taketh him up into an exceeding high mountain, and sheweth him all the kingdoms of the world, and the glory of them;
>
> And saith unto him, All these things will I give thee, if thou wilt fall down and worship me.
>
> Matthew 4:8,9

Jesus did not say that the devil was lying when he offered Him the nations of the world and its glory. But neither did He succumb to his temptation.

Jesus resisted the devil by the Word of God: **Then saith Jesus unto him, Get thee hence, Satan: for it is written, Thou shalt worship the Lord thy God, and him only shalt thou serve** (Matt. 4:10).

Jesus showed that the Word was the sword by which Christians overcome the devil.

Jesus also recognized that some forms of sickness are a spirit: **When Jesus saw that the people came running together, he rebuked the foul spirit, saying unto him, Thou dumb and deaf spirit, I charge thee, come out of him, and enter no more into him** (Mark 9:25).

Jesus called seizures, such as epilepsy, a spirit:

> Lord, have mercy on my son: for he is lunatick, and sore vexed: for ofttimes he falleth into the fire, and oft into the water.

> And I brought him to thy disciples, and they could not cure him.
>
> Then Jesus answered and said, O faithless and perverse generation, how long shall I be with you? how long shall I suffer you? bring him hither to me.
>
> And Jesus rebuked the devil; and he departed out of him: and the child was cured from that very hour.
>
> Matthew 17:15-18

The son spoken of here was also called a lunatic. These are symptoms which medical science may call sickness. Jesus Christ designated them as the work of evil spirits.

In the synagogue where Christ worshipped and read from the law of Moses, He discovered those who had evil spirits:

> And in the synagogue there was a man, which had a spirit of an unclean devil, and cried out with a loud voice,
>
> Saying, Let us alone; what have we to do with thee, thou Jesus of Nazareth? art thou come to destroy us? I know thee who thou art; the Holy One of God.
>
> And Jesus rebuked him, saying, Hold thy peace, and come out of him. And when the devil had thrown him in the midst, he came out of him, and hurt him not.
>
> Luke 4:33-35

The spirit cried out the identity of Jesus, that He was the Holy One of God. Christ silenced the man and commanded the spirit to come out of him. In anger the spirit threw the man violently, but Christ would not let it hurt him as he was forever loosed of its power.

I would like for you to notice that the possessed man did not cry out with a loud voice until Jesus got there. Those people sang their songs, said their prayers, read their scriptures, and the devil enjoyed it all. But when the power of God came on the scene, suddenly the devil became quite upset. Why? Because religious ceremony is no threat to him.

We can hold regular church services and demon-possessed people can sit right through them undisturbed. But when the glory of God is manifested and the Spirit of the Lord moves, the devil can't stand it.

That is why I stress so much the importance of exercising our divine authority over demons. As long as we confine our Christianity to religious observances, we pose no threat whatsoever to Satan and his kingdom. It is only when we come against him in the power and authority of Jesus Christ that we win any victories over him.

Satan can and does infiltrate the Church, and religious people are never even aware of it. They do not discern it until someone comes in with divine authority. You and I are to be that someone.

The Importance of Fasting and Prayer

Is fasting and praying important in exorcising demon spirits? Can some be cast out without fasting while others cannot?

Since Jesus Christ is our chief example and we are exhorted to follow Him, we should consider that the Bible repeatedly says that Christ fasted often. I personally believe that fasting is a source of spiritual strength and power.

Just before Christ's triumphant entry into His public ministry, He fasted for forty days: **And when he had fasted forty days and forty nights, he was afterward an hungred** (Matt. 4:2).

It seems that before the major experiences of His life, our Master did fast. For us today, it is very important to fast, especially before seeking to cast out some evil spirit.

We are taught that there are varying degrees of power among the demonic forces in the spirit world. After casting out the epileptic spirit from the boy who had suffered from seizures, Jesus told His disciples that they had not been able to cast it out because **...this kind goeth not out but by prayer and fasting** (Matt. 17:21). Therefore it is sure that there are certain spirits which will resist one until he has prepared himself for spiritual encounter.

Resisting the Devil

In James 4:7 we are told: **Submit yourselves therefore to God. Resist the devil, and he will flee from you.**

The Word of God is either true or not true. If we as Christians have authority to resist the devil, we must obey. The word *resist* is a military word. It indicates offensive action. It means to take the initiative.

If Christians actively, persistently, dogmatically and spiritually resist the devil, then the Bible says that he will flee. If the devil will run from us in terror, why should we Christians be afraid of him? How can he hurt us?

This is the positive side of Christian security and power. Let's stand firm in that security and use that power at our disposal to tear down the strongholds of Satan and to **set at liberty them that are bruised** (Luke 4:18).

20

What Happens to a Person After the Alien Entity Is Cast Out?

> When the unclean spirit is gone out of a man, he walketh through dry places, seeking rest; and finding none, he saith, I will return unto my house whence I came out.
>
> **Luke 11:24**

When we begin to exercise our power and authority to set people free from demon possession, it is important that we know what we are doing. Without sufficient knowledge and understanding of the world of the spirit, we run the risk of causing harm to those we deliver.

Setting people free is one thing, keeping them free is another. It is vitally important to teach a person how to remain free once he has been liberated.

There is an amazing revolution which takes place in a person who has been delivered from an alien entity. A new world of joy and peace opens up. He or she becomes normal in thinking and action. However, that person must respond to spiritual growth. To one person who had just been delivered, our Lord Jesus said, **Behold, thou art made whole: sin no more, lest a worse thing come unto thee** (John 5:14).

Let's examine some Biblical examples of people set free from demon possession to see what took place after their deliverance.

The First World Emperor

One of the most dramatic examples of what happens to a human who has been delivered from a foreign, non-human power and restored to his former normality, dignity and prosperity (propriety) is recorded in Daniel 4:28-37:

> All this came upon the king Nebuchadnezzar.
>
> At the end of twelve months he walked in the palace of the kingdom of Babylon.
>
> The king spake, and said, Is not this great Babylon, that I have built for the house of the kingdom by the might of my power, and for the honour of my majesty?
>
> While the word was in the king's mouth, there fell a voice from heaven, saying, O king Nebuchadnezzar, to thee it is spoken; The kingdom is departed from thee.
>
> And they shall drive thee from men, and thy dwelling shall be with the beasts of the field: they shall make thee to eat grass as oxen, and seven times shall pass over thee, until thou know that the most High ruleth in the kingdom of men, and giveth it to whomsoever he will.
>
> The same hour was the thing fulfilled upon Nebuchadnezzar: and he was driven from men, and did eat grass as oxen, and his body was wet with the dew of heaven, till his hairs were grown like eagles' feathers, and his nails like birds' claws.
>
> And at the end of the days I Nebuchadnezzar lifted up mine eyes unto heaven, and mine understanding returned unto me, and I blessed the most High, and I praised and honoured him that liveth for ever, whose dominion is an everlasting dominion, and his kingdom is from generation to generation:
>
> And all the inhabitants of the earth are reputed as nothing: and he doeth according to his will in the

army of heaven, and among the inhabitants of the earth: and none can stay his hand, or say unto him, What doest thou?

At the same time my reason returned unto me; and for the glory of my kingdom, mine honour and brightness returned unto me; and my counsellors and my lords sought unto me; and I was established in my kingdom, and excellent majesty was added unto me.

Now I Nebuchadnezzar praise and extol and honour the King of heaven, all whose works are truth, and his ways judgment: and those that walk in pride he is able to abase.

This is a mighty declaration of the reaction of a once-proud monarch whose mind was restored after having been reduced to the state of an imbecile. For seven long years he had lived with animals and had eaten grass like an ox. Then he was completely restored by the power of God. He gave deep praises to the King of heaven, the Jehovah God of Daniel and of Shadrach, Meshach and Abednego.

Notice that after his recovery, he gave himself, not to praising heathen deities or gods made of silver, gold or stone, but to magnifying the true God to whom he attributed all honor, praise and glory. Before his possession by demons, the king had exalted only himself. But when his mind was restored unto him, he recognized the true Source of all his honor and brightness. He then had a right attitude toward God. He gave God the honor and glory that was due Him as the giver of every good and perfect gift.

What a colossal lesson humanity ought to learn from this story.

Mary of Magdala

We have already examined the story of Mary Magdalene who was delivered of seven devils. (Luke 8:2.) We noted that after her deliverance, she became a true disciple of Jesus. She financially supported His ministry. (Luke 8:3.) She was one of the few who followed Jesus to the cross. (John 19:25.) She came to the tomb to anoint Jesus' body. (Mark 16:1.) She was the first to see the risen Lord and the first evangelist of the Resurrection. (Mark 16:9; John 20:18.)

This too should serve as an example to us of the kind of attitude and behavior we might expect from a person who has been miraculously delivered from the power of Satan.

One Becomes Eight

But there is another Biblical example given by Jesus Himself which illustrates what happens to a delivered person who does not take care to preserve his liberty in Christ.

> When the unclean spirit is gone out of a man, he walketh through dry places, seeking rest, and findeth none.
>
> Then he saith, I will return into my house from whence I came out; and when he is come, he findeth it empty, swept, and garnished.
>
> Then goeth he, and taketh with himself seven other spirits more wicked than himself, and they enter in and dwell there: and the last state of that man is worse than the first. Even so shall it be also unto this wicked generation.
>
> **Matthew 12:43-45**

This man was possessed by one alien entity at first. Then that evil spirit was cast out of him. Jesus says that the spirit walked in dry places (a wilderness area where humans do not live), seeking rest. This is a revelation.

That spirit went through a wilderness seeking someone to possess, but not finding any. So the spirit said to himself, "I will return to my house, from whence I came out." Notice that the demon called his former abode his "house"! This proves that alien entities do indeed seek to possess humans and do seek to take control of them for their own purposes. If the demon cannot locate another person to possess, he will try to go back into the one he was cast out of. That is the primary point of this lesson.

So the evil spirit came back to his former "residence." He found it empty—not full of the Holy Spirit or the Word of God. He found it swept and cleaned. The bad things had been cleared out. But that was not enough to keep him out.

To empty a person of bad things is not sufficient. It is exceedingly important to get that person filled with the right things, the things of God. Many people will not follow after Jesus for the simple reason they haven't been taught that once they have been emptied of something bad, then they must be filled with something good.

It is so easy to have a Sunday morning religion and not have any spiritual authority, strength or joy. It's easy to have religion and not have Jesus. We must never permit ourselves to get into such a situation.

Since this man was empty on the inside, the evil entity saw that there was a possibility of his returning. For security he invited seven other spirits, who had no one to possess, to form a league together, and all eight possessed the man. These seven spirits were more wicked than the first.

Thus Jesus teaches that there are degrees of wickedness in alien entities. He also taught that they all entered into the man, dwelled there and made themselves at home, demonstrating that one person can be possessed of multiple entities. Verse 45 says that the last state of that man was worse than the first.

Every rational person should thank God for his sanity. When any person receives a miracle of restoration from Jesus, he has a direct responsibility of appreciation to live a life pleasing to God and His Christ. The man Jesus told about missed the mark!

The Bible says in Ephesians 5:18: **And be not drunk with wine, wherein is excess; but be filled with the Spirit.** The Word of God declares that bitter waters and sweet waters cannot come out of the same fountain. If you are full of God, you are not full of evil. You cannot be full of God and full of the devil at the same time. Neither can you be half and half. Jesus said that a house divided against itself cannot stand. (Matt. 12:25.) You cannot remain half good and half evil with these two forces fighting within you.

Either you have Jesus in your heart, or you don't.

If you have Christ in your heart, then you have power and authority to cast out evil entities.

The Miracle of the Demoniac of Gadara

Finally, we come to one of the most amazing stories on record illustrating what can happen to a person set free. We have already read the account of the deliverance of the demoniac of Gadara. Now let's examine his story step by step.

> **And there followed him (Jesus) great multitudes of people from Galilee, and from Decapolis, and from Jerusalem, and from Judaea, and from beyond Jordan.**
>
> **Matthew 4:25**

> **And they came over unto the other side of the sea, into the country of the Gadarenes.**
>
> **Mark 5:1**

This man was from Decapolis, an area made up of ten cities, in the land of the Gadarenes. As such, he was a pagan and lived in a pagan environment.

> **And when he was come out of the ship, immediately there met him out of the tombs a man with an unclean spirit,**
>
> **Who had his dwelling among the tombs; and no man could bind him, no, not with chains:**
>
> **Because that he had been often bound with fetters and chains, and the chains had been plucked asunder by him, and the fetters broken in pieces: neither could any man tame him.**
>
> **And always, night and day, he was in the mountains, and in the tombs, crying, and cutting himself with stones.**
>
> **Mark 5:2-5**

Somehow this man had become possessed of a legion of alien spirits. When Jesus discovered him, he was naked and wild.

> **But when he saw Jesus afar off, he ran and worshipped him,**
>
> **And cried with a loud voice, and said, What have I to do with thee, Jesus, thou Son of the most high God? I adjure thee by God, that thou torment me not.**

For he said unto him, Come out of the man, thou unclean spirit.

And he asked him, What is thy name? And he answered, saying, My name is Legion: for we are many.

And he besought him much that he would not send them away out of the country.

Now there was there nigh unto the mountains a great herd of swine feeding.

And all the devils besought him, saying, Send us into the swine, that we may enter into them.

And forthwith Jesus gave them leave. And the unclean spirits went out, and entered into the swine: and the herd ran violently down a steep place into the sea, (they were about two thousand;) and were choked in the sea.

Mark 5:6-13

So then Jesus delivered the demoniac by sending the legion of evil spirits out of him and into a herd of swine.

And they that fed the swine fled, and told it in the city, and in the country. And they went out to see what it was that was done.

And they come to Jesus, and see him that was possessed with the devil, and had the legion, sitting, and clothed, and in his right mind: and they were afraid.

And they that saw it told them how it befell to him that was possessed with the devil, and also concerning the swine.

And they began to pray him to depart out of their coasts.

And when he was come into the ship, he that had been possessed with the devil prayed him that he might be with him.

Mark 5:14-18

Notice that after this man was delivered, his first reaction was to request discipleship. He asked Jesus if he might go with Him. Like Mary Magdalene, he wanted to spend the rest of his life following and serving the One Who had set him free.

> **Howbeit Jesus suffered him not, but saith unto him, Go home to thy friends, and tell them how great things the Lord hath done for thee, and hath had compassion on thee.**
>
> **Mark 5:19**

Instead of allowing the man to come with Him as he requested, Jesus sent him back to witness to his own people. He was to testify to those who knew of his former possession by alien entities.

> **And he departed, and began to publish in Decapolis how great things Jesus had done for him: and all men did marvel.**
>
> **Mark 5:20**

The former demoniac did as he was instructed by Jesus. As a result of his testimony, people marveled at what Jesus had done for him. He gathered together an enormous crowd to see and hear Jesus.

> **And again, departing from the coasts of Tyre and Sidon, he (Jesus) came unto the sea of Galilee, through the midst of the coasts of Decapolis.**
>
> **Mark 7:31**

Some time later, Jesus returns to this area. Whereas before, the people had asked Him to depart from their country, now as a result of the witness of this man multitudes were ready to receive Him.

> **And they bring unto him one that was deaf, and had an impediment in his speech; and they beseech him to put his hand upon him...**

211

And straightway his ears were opened, and the string of his tongue was loosed, and he spake plain.

And he charged them that they should tell no man: but the more he charged them, so much the more a great deal they published it;

And were beyond measure astonished, saying, He hath done all things well: he maketh both the deaf to hear, and the dumb to speak.

Mark 7:32,35-37

So now many are taught, healed and blessed of the Lord because this one man testified to his miraculous deliverance from demon possession. Those who were previously afraid and opposed to Jesus are bringing to Him others to be set free. They too are praising Jesus for His wonderful works and spreading the news of it everywhere.

Whereas one man who was delivered from an alien entity remained empty, thus allowing himself to become seven times more demon possessed than before, this man was filled with a spirit of gratitude and praise to God, thus allowing himself to become a multitude.

In those days the multitude being very great, and having nothing to eat, Jesus called his disciples unto him, and saith unto them,

I have compassion on the multitude, because they have now been with me three days, and have nothing to eat:

And if I send them away fasting to their own houses, they will faint by the way: for divers of them came from far.

And his disciples answered him, From whence can a man satisfy these men with bread here in the wilderness?

> And he asked them, How many loaves have ye? And they said, Seven.
>
> And he commanded the people to sit down on the ground: and he took the seven loaves, and gave thanks, and brake, and gave to his disciples to set before them; and they did set them before the people.
>
> And they had a few small fishes: and he blessed, and commanded to set them also before them.
>
> So they did eat, and were filled: and they took up of the broken meat that was left seven baskets.
>
> And they that had eaten were about four thousand: and he sent them away.
>
> **Mark 8:1-9**

Four thousand people ate all they desired, and at Jesus' command seven baskets of fragments were gathered up!

What a witness to the results of setting a man free from an alien possession. It was a "one-man-plus-the-Holy-Ghost" revival!

We should not only set people free, we should take care to see what happens to them after their deliverance. When you set someone free, then you have an obligation to that person to teach him or her the Word of God about how to remain free. Don't allow them to fall back into demon possession or oppression. Take it as your responsibility to help them stay free of Satan's bondage.

21

The Antichrist

For many deceivers are entered into the world, who confess not that Jesus Christ is come in the flesh. This is a deceiver and an antichrist.

2 John 7

There has been much discussion and debate about the person designated in the Bible as the Antichrist. Different people have different ideas about the subject, but actually the Bible is quite clear in this regard.

What Is the Antichrist?

In order to define the Antichrist, let's first consider what he is not. Despite what many people may say, he is not just a system, either political or philosophical. *Antichrist* is not a metaphor or a rhetorical form of speech, nor is he an influence projected by this age. Antichrist is not just a spirit of anarchy in the world, though that may exist and indeed does. Antichrist is not a distorted creature with a head like a monster.

The being referred to by the Bible as the Antichrist is specifically a man, a human possessed by an alien entity.

Broadly speaking, an antichrist is anyone who is possessed of a spirit other than that of Christ. The person designated in history to become the Antichrist will be a corporeal person, just like you and me. Yet he will

215

be totally possessed of an alien entity, possessed as no other person in the history of the world.

He will be the number one person on the face of this earth during the last days. His strength will be so great that he will rule the major part of the world. He will set himself up as a god. He will have statues or idols made in his likeness and anyone refusing to bow down and worship these idols will be executed.

Antichrist is Satan's answer to God. God produced Jesus the Savior and the devil will produce a counterfeit savior called Antichrist. The world will decide which savior to follow, God's Savior or the devil's. Unquestionably, the global stage is set for the diabolical appearing of this person the Bible calls the Man of Sin. (2 Thess. 2:3.)

This does not mean that he will be called the Antichrist by people. His title might be something like the Secretary-General of the United Nations, or the President of the European Common Market, or any number of other designations such as Leader, or even Big Brother (as in George Orwell's novel, *1984*).

What God calls a thing and what man calls it may be different. But what God calls it is the essence of it, the true nature and spirit of it. And the nature and spirit of this man will be satanic, anti-Christ.

Why Will There Be an Antichrist?

When mankind refuses God's Christ, our Savior, there is no alternative but to receive the devil's christ, or Antichrist.

This generation has planted the seed of universal moral breakdown, of hatred and violence, of witchcraft and heathen worship. God has been relegated to the background.

This generation says it has no need for God, that it can get along without God. They oppose expressing faith in God, or worship. Parents want their children to grow up without the fear of God and to give their minds to television and every other kind of uncleanness. They know nothing of God's laws or judgments.

> And even as they did not like to retain God in their knowledge, God gave them over to a reprobate mind, to do those things which are not convenient;
>
> Being filled with all unrighteousness, fornication, wickedness, covetousness, maliciousness; full of envy, murder, debate, deceit, malignity; whisperers,
>
> Backbiters, haters of God, despiteful, proud, boasters, inventors of evil things, disobedient to parents,
>
> Without understanding, covenant breakers, without natural affection, implacable, unmerciful:
>
> Who knowing the judgment of God, that they which commit such things are worthy of death, not only do the same, but have pleasure in them that do them.
>
> **Romans 1:28-32**

This passage was written nearly 2,000 years ago, yet you would think it had been written just yesterday. This is a picture of this generation: people of reprobate minds doing things which God has expressly forbidden under penalty of death, with no feeling of guilt or remorse, and no desire to turn to God for His forgiveness and salvation.

Modern parents do not realize that humans are either slaves to God or to the devil. The horrible pits of Satan are drugs, sex and alcohol. Today's parents think their children are beautiful and sophisticated, but actually they have exploding minds filled with every kind of lewdness and filth brought on by drugs, alcohol and pornography. Ours is a generation of rebels against all forms of authority, including God's.

All this indicates that our modern world is rapidly preparing itself for the appearance of the supreme antagonist, the prophesied archenemy of God. Our generation is being constantly conditioned emotionally, spiritually, morally, economically and politically for the appearance and rule of a world dictator—a global ruler.

Modern society, worldwide, is clamoring for a superman of destiny to lead them—one with potential to lift it out of distress, discouragement and destruction. The Antichrist will present himself as that champion.

What Will the Antichrist Be Like?

First of all, the Antichrist will be a perfect replica of his generation. No generation of history will ever have been more fully represented by a perfect type of itself as will the generation of the Antichrist. He will completely fulfill the popular conception of the ideal man of his day. He will not seem to be a strange person to the millions of humanity who will adore and follow him. He will be a perfect reflection of the life, soul and spirit of the people of his time, of his followers and admirers.

Secondly, the Antichrist will possess the characteristics of all the great empires of time:

And I stood upon the sand of the sea, and saw a beast rise up out of the sea, having seven heads and ten horns, and upon his horns ten crowns, and upon his heads the name of blasphemy.

And the beast which I saw was like unto a leopard, and his feet were as the feet of a bear, and his mouth as the mouth of a lion: and the dragon gave him his power, and his seat, and great authority.

And I saw one of his heads as it were wounded to death; and his deadly wound was healed: and all the world wondered after the beast.

And they worshipped the dragon which gave power unto the beast: and they worshipped the beast, saying, Who is like unto the beast? who is able to make war with him?

And there was given unto him a mouth speaking great things and blasphemies; and power was given unto him to continue forty and two months.

And he opened his mouth in blasphemy against God, to blaspheme his name, and his tabernacle, and them that dwell in heaven.

And it was given unto him to make war with the saints, and to overcome them: and power was given him over all kindreds, and tongues, and nations.

And all that dwell upon the earth shall worship him, whose names are not written in the book of life of the Lamb slain from the foundation of the world.

If any man have an ear, let him hear.

He that leadeth into captivity shall go into captivity: he that killeth with the sword must be killed with the sword. Here is the patience and faith of the saints.

Revelation 13:1-10

From this passage we see that the Antichrist will rise from the sea, which represents the mass of humanity, the common people. He will not come from the nobility or from the upper class of society. He will be a commander who rises up from the common people.

We also see that he will have names of blasphemy and shall hate God.

There are four images given in this passage which relate to this man:

1. A leopard—representing the Grecian Empire

> **After this I beheld, and lo another, like a leopard, which had upon the back of it four wings of a fowl; the beast had also four heads; and dominion was given to it.**
>
> **Daniel 7:6**

2. The feet of a bear—representing the Persian Empire

3. The mouth of a lion—representing the Babylonian Empire

4. The dragon—representing Satan, the alien entity which possesses him.

> **Neither shall he regard the God of his fathers, nor the desire of women, nor regard any god: for he shall magnify himself above all.**
>
> **Daniel 11:37**

The Antichrist may be a Jewish man or a man of some other religion, but whatever his religious background, he will not regard or respect the God of his fathers. It is generally understood that *nor the desire of women* means that the Antichrist will be an avowed homosexual; he will have announced himself as such.

In Luke 17:28-30 Jesus describes what it will be like in the last days before His return to earth: **Likewise**

also as it was in the days of Lot...Even thus shall it be in the day when the Son of man is revealed. In Sodom, Lot's hometown, it was popular to be a homosexual, or sodomite.

The Antichrist will lead the world in immorality. The people will praise him for being brazen in his sin and for being uninhibited. Psychiatry will no doubt label him as the perfectly adapted man, a role model for the age.

The Antichrist will be hailed as a miracle man. He will do phenomenal things. He will produce lying wonders to convince the world of his power and divinity. He will have a deadly head wound which will be "miraculously" healed, turning many people to faith in him.

Daniel 8:23 tells us, **And in the latter time of their kingdom, when the transgressors are come to the full, a king of fierce countenance, and understanding dark sentences, shall stand up.**

By his cunning and deceit this man, the Antichrist, will elevate himself to the position of world leader. He will become respected and feared. Everyone in the world will see his "fierce countenance" by television and be afraid of him. Daniel 9:26,27 refers to his reign, calling him "the prince that shall come." He will become an object of worship:

> **And they worshipped the dragon which gave power unto the beast** (the Antichrist)**: and they worshipped the beast, saying, Who is like unto the beast? who is able to make war with him?**
>
> **And the first went, and poured out his vial upon the earth; and there fell a noisome and grievous sore**

upon the men which had the mark of the beast, and upon them which worshipped his image.

Revelation 13:4; 16:2

How Can the Antichrist Be Identified?

The Bible says that the Antichrist will be marked with a number:

Here is wisdom. Let him that hath understanding count the number of the beast: for it is the number of man; and his number is Six hundred threescore and six.

Revelation 13:18

There are some people who find the Antichrist everywhere they look. They seem to spend their time scouring around, trying to come up with the number 666. It doesn't matter how many times you see that number today. Until the Antichrist himself comes upon the scene, this number will have no significance. The true significance of it will be when no one else in the world is allowed to have it but the Antichrist. When he is revealed, then he will claim sole ownership of it as his own private, exclusive and identifying number.

Who Is the Antichrist?

Now we beseech you, brethren, by the coming of our Lord Jesus Christ, and by our gathering together unto him,

That ye be not soon shaken in mind, or be troubled, neither by spirit, nor by word, nor by letter as from us, as that the day of Christ is at hand.

Let no man deceive you by any means: for that day shall not come, except there come a falling away first, and that man of sin be revealed, the son of perdition.

2 Thessalonians 2:1-3

The Antichrist is called the son of perdition by the Bible. *Perdition* means a state of lostness. Just as God is salvation, Satan is lostness or perdition. The Antichrist will be the son of perdition. He will be like his father, just as Jesus was like His Father. And just as Jesus was filled with His Father's Spirit, so will the Antichrist be filled with the spirit of his father, the devil.

Just as Satan deceived man in the Garden of Eden, so this Antichrist will deceive mankind in the last days. He will gather unto himself a huge following and lead them in rebellion and warfare against the saints of God.

Now the saints against whom he will be warring are not the Church. They are the people who will have been turned to God during the Great Tribulation. The Church will be gone from the earth by that time. They will be dwelling in heaven.

How Long Will the Antichrist Rule?

The Antichrist will be in power for some seven years. He is going to frighten the whole world into submission unto him. His mouth will be like the mouth of Nebuchadnezzar the king before his repentance. (Dan. 4:28-30.)

Antichrist will reign as supreme ruler during the first forty-two months or three and one-half years of the Great Tribulation. His fierce battle with Christ, or God, will be during the last three and one-half years. During this time plagues and judgments shall be brought upon him and his followers. Hail stones weighing 100 pounds will fall. The sun shall scorch men. Water will be turned to blood. Yet these judgments will not turn men to God.

How Will the Antichrist End?

And then shall that Wicked be revealed, whom the Lord shall consume with the spirit of his mouth, and shall destroy with the brightness of his coming:

Even him, whose coming is after the working of Satan with all power and signs and lying wonders,

And with all deceivableness of unrighteousness in them that perish; because they received not the love of the truth, that they might be saved.

And for this cause God shall send them strong delusion, that they should believe a lie:

That they all might be damned who believed not the truth, but had pleasure in unrighteousness.

2 Thessalonians 2:8-12

The Antichrist will be destroyed by the Lord Jesus when He comes in power and majesty from on high. Anyone and everyone who has taken the mark of the beast (the mark of the Antichrist), all who have knelt before his image to worship him, who have received the spirit of Antichrist, will be damned. There is no hope of salvation for them.

I am glad that you and I as Christians will not be here to have to suffer all these horrible things. The Bride of Christ will already have been caught away. **Wherefore comfort one another with these words** (1 Thess. 4:18).

22

God's Final Word on Alien Entities

And there was war in heaven: Michael and his angels fought against the dragon; and the dragon fought and his angels,

And prevailed not; neither was their place found any more in heaven.

And the great dragon was cast out, that old serpent, called the Devil, and Satan, which deceiveth the whole world: he was cast out into the earth, and his angels were cast out with him.

And I heard a loud voice saying in heaven, Now is come salvation, and strength, and the kingdom of our God, and the power of his Christ: for the accuser of our brethren is cast down, which accused them before our God day and night.

And they overcame him by the blood of the Lamb, and by the word of their testimony; and they loved not their lives unto the death.

Therefore rejoice, ye heavens, and ye that dwell in them. Woe to the inhabiter of the earth and of the sea! for the devil is come down unto you, having great wrath, because he knoweth that he hath but a short time.

Revelation 12:7-12

The devil, called in Revelation 10:10 the ''accuser of the brethren,'' was cast out of heaven, down to the earth, and his angels were cast out with him. Right now, the devil reigns as the prince of the power of the air. He rules in an area that is the depth of the atmosphere around this planet, a limited realm.

Through the disobedience and fall of Adam, Satan stole from man his rightful dominion over this earth. Before that time, Satan had no claim upon it.

Satan is now the prince of the air, but there will come a time when he will no longer have that position. He will be cast down from the heavenly place, down to the earth's surface, he and all his angels. The seven-year period during which he reigns over the earth in the form of the beast, or the Antichrist, will be known as the Great Tribulation. It is at the end of that period that God will completely destroy all the forces of alien entities. They will be put into a bottomless pit, from which Satan will later be loosed for a time before being finally cast into the lake of fire with his demons and followers. There they will all suffer punishment forever and ever.

From Genesis to Revelation God spoke of, described and warned of alien entities. He told man where these entities came from, what they will do, and finally, their ultimate destiny.

Entities Know Their End

In Mark 1:23-26 we read where Jesus encountered a demon-possessed man:

> And there was in their synagogue a man with an unclean spirit; and he cried out,
>
> Saying, Let us alone; what have we to do with thee, thou Jesus of Nazareth? art thou come to destroy us? I know thee who thou art, the Holy One of God.

And Jesus rebuked him, saying, Hold thy peace, and come out of him.

And when the unclean spirit had torn him, and cried with a loud voice, he came out of him.

In Matthew 8:28,29 we find the account of Jesus' encounter with the demoniacs of the Gergesenes:

And when he was come to the other side into the country of the Gergesenes, there met him two possessed with devils, coming out of the tombs, exceeding fierce, so that no man might pass by that way.

And, behold, they cried out, saying, What have we to do with thee, Jesus, thou Son of God? art thou come hither to torment us before the time?

Notice what the evil spirits said to Jesus in these two instances: "Have You come to destroy us, to torment us before the time?" These entities know their fate; they are very much aware of the terrible destiny that awaits them. Revelation 12:12 points out that Satan comes down to the earth in **great wrath, because he knoweth that he hath but a short time.**

These alien entities know that they have been disobedient to God. They remember that at one time they made up the choir of heaven, how they praised God before His glorious throne.

As we have seen, there were three archangels in heaven: Michael, the military leader of heaven; Gabriel, the communications angel; and Lucifer, who was in charge of the heavenly choir, the music, singing and praise in heaven. The majesty of the great and mighty God flowed through him to all the rest of heaven.

It was Lucifer who exalted himself, saying, **I will exalt my throne above the stars of God** (Is. 14:13).

When he and his followers were cast out of heaven, there was left an emptiness in one third of heaven. The Lord Jesus spoke to the Father God and said, "Father, I would like to bring in something new to replace these fallen angels. I would like to bring in redeemed persons who have been saved, transformed and brought out of the kingdom of the one who was cast out, and translated into My Kingdom. They shall stand in this place and praise You forever and ever and ever."

So the Lord came and purchased us by His own blood, that we might fill that void in the heart and center of heaven. Throughout all eternity, we will lead the singing and praise to God. We have thus taken the place of honor and glory formerly occupied by Satan and his angelic host. This is just one more reason the devil is against us. He knows that we are going to have his place of honor in heaven for eternity.

Satan knows where he came from. He knows what he has lost and who has taken his place in heaven. He also knows his destiny, his end. That's why the demons said to Jesus, "Don't destroy us! Don't torment us before our time!"

There is a time coming for Satan. We are this very moment arriving at the conclusion of what man calls time. At that point in eternity, God will begin His judgment, which will be an eternal one.

Inter-World Warfare

We observe cosmic warfare. We do believe and accept Biblical revelation. We find that God has become angry with alien entities. There is a final day of judgment awaiting them. They will suffer eternally for their rebellion against God.

God hates rebellion and a rebellious spirit in any form. That is why, as we have said, He deals so harshly with witchcraft, because His Word says that witchcraft is a form of rebellion against Him. Those who practice witchcraft, whether they realize it or not, are taking part in rebellion against the Most High. They are looking to alien entities for protection, guidance and help, rather than to the Almighty, their Creator. Consciously or unconsciously, they are joining Satan and his demons in their efforts to usurp the power and position of Almighty God. And that, God will not allow.

There is a cosmic warfare going on for control of this universe. And we as Christians must be very careful about which side we take in this monumental conflict.

Satan Cast Down Upon the Earth

Michael is God's archangel of war. The battle is in the Second Heaven, where Satan is the "prince and power." Michael uses his angels to do battle with the devil and his angels. Michael defeats the alien entities. He removes Satan from his position of princeship, and there is found no place for him in the air. Satan will be cast down upon the earth where he will have his headquarters. His entities will be cast down with him.

There will be great wrath for a short time, which period the Bible calls the Great Tribulation. Woe to the inhabitants of the earth during that time! Satanic wrath will be worse then than ever before in history. This will endure for only a relatively short time because Satan's end is near.

Then the Lord Jesus Christ will return to this earth. This time His coming will not be to take away His

Bride, the Church. That event will already have taken place seven years before. This time He will be returning **with His saints** to avenge His name upon the Antichrist. (Jude 14.) There will follow a final battle, the defeat of the Antichrist, and the casting down of Satan and his hosts. Then will begin the Kingdom reign, during which time Christ will reign in peace upon the earth for 1,000 years.

The King of Entities Judged

What is going to happen to alien entities in the end? We thank God they are going to be entombed forever. They will not be bothering anybody anymore.

> And I saw an angel come down from heaven, having the key of the bottomless pit and a great chain in his hand.
>
> And he laid hold on the dragon, that old serpent, which is the Devil, and Satan, and bound him a thousand years,
>
> And cast him into the bottomless pit, and shut him up, and set a seal upon him, that he should deceive the nations no more, till the thousand years should be fulfilled: and after that he must be loosed a little season...
>
> And when the thousand years are expired, Satan shall be loosed out of his prison...
>
> And the devil that deceived them was cast into the lake of fire and brimstone, where the beast and the false prophet are, and shall be tormented day and night for ever and ever.
>
> Revelation 20:1-3,7,10

This is the ultimate end of this one who is the alien entity, the one who has hurt, deceived and possessed people through history. His end is eternal damnation in the lake of fire. Those who have served him will share the same fate. But those who have served God will receive the **crown of life, which the Lord hath promised to them that love him** (James 1:12). A crown denotes kingship. As faithful Christians, as the sons and daughters of God, we will reign with Jesus forever and ever!

God's Final Word to Believers About Alien Entities

Finally, we believers are taught by the Word of God how to deal with Satan and his demons.

1. We put on God's armor to fight him:

> Put on the whole armour of God, that ye may be able to stand against the wiles of the devil.
>
> **Ephesians 6:11**

2. We give no place to him:

> Neither give place to the devil.
>
> **Ephesians 4:27**

3. We know his devices:

> Lest Satan should get an advantage of us: for we are not ignorant of his devices.
>
> **2 Corinthians 2:11**

4. Because of this we resist him:

> Submit yourselves therefore to God. Resist the devil, and he will flee from you.
>
> **James 4:7**
>
> Be sober, be vigilant; because your adversary the devil, as a roaring lion, walketh about, seeking whom he may devour:

231

Whom resist steadfast in the faith, knowing that the same afflictions are accomplished in your brethren that are in the world.

1 Peter 5:8,9

5. Then we overcome him by God's Spirit:

This I say then, Walk in the Spirit, and ye shall not fulfill the lust of the flesh....

If we live in the Spirit, let us also walk in the Spirit.

Galatians 5:16,25

There is therefore now no condemnation to them which are in Christ Jesus, who walk not after the flesh, but after the Spirit....

For ye have not received the spirit of bondage again to fear; but ye have received the Spirit of adoption, whereby we cry, Abba, Father.

Romans 8:1,15

6. We overcome him by the Blood of Jesus:

And they overcame him by the blood of the Lamb, and by the word of their testimony; and they loved not their lives unto the death.

Revelation 12:11

MY CHALLENGE TO YOU

If Jesus should come today, would you be ready? If you are not sure, I invite you to receive Jesus as your Savior now. You will be filled with hope and peace that only Jesus can offer.

Pray out loud with me right now:

"Dear Lord Jesus, I am a sinner. I do believe that you died and rose from the dead to save me from my sins. I want to be with you in heaven forever. God, forgive me of all my sins that I have committed against you. I here and now open my heart to you and ask you to come into my heart and life and be my personal Savior. Amen."

When you pray the Sinner's Prayer and mean it, He will come in instantly. You are now a child of God and you have been transferred from the devil's dominion to the kingdom of God. Read I John 1:9 and Colossians 1:13. A wonderful peace and joy will fill your soul.

Please write and tell me what Jesus has done for you. I will send you a little pamphlet titled, "So You're Born Again!" Mail your letter to: **Lester Sumrall,** P.O. Box 12, South Bend, Indiana 46624.

WHO WE ARE

Lester Sumrall is founder and chairman of a worldwide missionary outreach, The Lester Sumrall Evangelistic Association (LeSEA). Respected throughout the world as a missionary statesman, Dr. Sumrall has raised up churches and taught the Word of God for almost sixty years. In addition, he maintains headquarters for LeSEA Global Feed the Hungry, "The End-Time Joseph Program," and LeSEA Broadcasting (international radio and television) in South Bend, Indiana where he resides with his wife, Louise. He is pastor of Christian Center Cathedral of Praise. Also involved in the ministry are three married sons: Frank, Stephen and Peter.

Dr. Sumrall is the prolific author of approximately a hundred and fifty books and teaching syllabi, founder and president of World Harvest Bible College, president of Indiana Christian University, and television host on LeSEA Alive and The Lester Sumrall Teaching Series (program seen around the world).

LeSEA Broadcasting, Inc. owns and operates to date five television stations: WHMB TV-40 Indianapolis, WHME TV-46 South Bend, KWHB TV-47 Tulsa, KWHE TV-14 Honolulu, WHKE TV-55 Kenosha, and has a construction permit for KWHD TV-53 Denver.

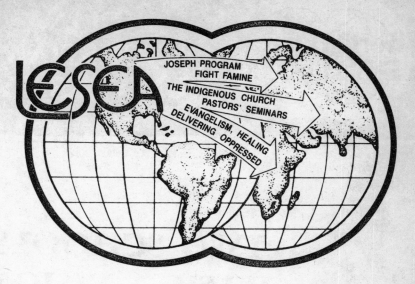

LeSEA

JOSEPH PROGRAM
FIGHT FAMINE

THE INDIGENOUS CHURCH
PASTORS' SEMINARS

EVANGELISM, HEALING
DELIVERING OPPRESSED

GLOBAL
FEED-THE-HUNGRY PROGRAM

You are invited to join LeSEA's End-Time Joseph Program which offers emergency help to Christians who live in areas plagued by poverty or famine.

While he was in Israel with a group of pilgrims, the Lord asked Dr. Sumrall to initiate a global program to combat hunger and he was told in detail how to tackle such a herculean task. God declared that the aggressive attack against the forces of evil should be three-pronged. How can this be done?

In conjunction with the feeding programs, seminars will be held when the people are ministered to spiritually. We will pray for the sick and deliver those in bondage. Pastors will then be given food and other supplies which they will distribute among their own congregations. This will elevate the pastor in the eyes of their people.

We are looking for 10,000 pastors to challenge world hunger by including "Feed the Hungry" in their missionary giving. For more information, write:

FEED THE HUNGRY, South Bend, IN
46680-7777 USA

Let us hear from you today. We must act now! Tomorrow may be too late!

World Harvest Bible College

INDIANA CHRISTIAN UNIVERSITY

TWO SCHOOLS WITH A VISION

Running with the vision of winning a million souls to Christ.
Dr. Lester Sumrall
Founder & President

Very highest academic standards

Investment return; top-quality education at bottom-dollar tuition

Spiritual emphasis—Full Gospel

Interaction—highly personalized faculty-student relationship

On the job training while in school

Nationally and internationally known guest teachers

Approved for Veteran Training
A.A. and B.A. Degrees

WORLD HARVEST

World Harvest Magazine is Lester Sumrall's pulpit to the world. This bi-monthly magazine contains faith-building articles and reports of what God is doing through LeSEA Ministries worldwide.

For your free copy, write —

World Harvest Magazine, P.O. Box 12, South Bend, Indiana, and ask to be added to the mailing list.

BOOKS BY DR. LESTER SUMRALL

- Adventuring With Christ
- My Story To His Glory
- Take It—It's Yours
- Gifts & Ministries Of The Holy Spirit
- Alien Entities
- Battle Of The Ages
- Beyond Anger And Pity
- Conscience—The Scales Of Eternal Justice
- Demons The Answer Book
- Bitten By Devils
- Ecstasy—Finding Joy In Living
- Faith To Change The World
- Faith Under Siege; The Life of Abraham
- Faith-Filled Words (Frank Sumrall)
- Fishers Of Men
- Gates Of Hell
- Genesis—Crucible Of The Universe
- Hostility
- Hypnotism—Divine Or Demonic
- Imagination—Hidden Force Of Human Potential
- I Predict 2000 A.D.
- Jerusalem, Where Empires Die—
  Will America Die At Jerusalem?
- Jihad—The Holy War
- Living Free
- Making Life Count
- Miracles Don't Just Happen
- 101 Questions & Answers On Demon Power
- Paul—Man Of The Millennia
- Run With The Vision
- Secrets Of Answered Prayer
- Sixty Things God Said About Sex
- Supernatural Principalities & Powers
- 20 Years Of "I Predict"
- The Mystery Of Immortality
- The Making Of A Champion
- The Names Of God
- The Promises Of God
- The Reality Of Angels
- The Stigma Of Calvary
- The Total Man
- The Will—The Potent Force Of The Universe
- The Human Body
- The Human Soul
- The Human Spirit
- Trajectory Of Faith—Joseph
- Three Habitations Of Devils
- Unprovoked Murder
- Victory And Dominion Over Fear
- You Can Conquer GRIEF Before It Conquers You

LeSEA PUBLISHING COMPANY, INC.

P.O. Box 12, South Bend, Indiana 46624

THREE HABITATIONS OF DEVILS

There are three areas spoken of in God's Word regarding the habitations of devils. Demons can dwell in nations, cities and individual beings, human or animal. Empires and nations have given themselves over to the worship of devils, becoming devil-infested. Ancient cities, as well as modern ones, practice Satan worship. Finally, humans have yielded themselves to the devil that he might possess them.

The great challenge of this age and hour is for the believer, using the power of Jesus' name, to defeat and destroy all the works of the devil.

THE MYSTERY OF IMMORTALITY

Immortality is one of the hottest debated subjects of our time. Communists, infidels, rationalists, evolotionists and humanists all agree that there is no life after death.

Oriental religions teach reincarnation, while Catholicism believes in purgatory, an intermediary place where man is purged from his sins before entering heaven.

What does the Bible teach about the eternalness of man? Let's get acquainted with life and immortality. Nothing is so exciting as a probe into the mystery of immortality.

Each 64-page book: REG. $1.95   **NOW $1.49**